# No More Summer-Reading Loss

# DEAR READERS,

Much like the diet phenomenon *Eat This, Not That*, this series aims to replace some existing practices with approaches that are more effective—healthier, if you will—for our students. We hope to draw attention to practices that have little support in research or professional wisdom and offer alternatives that have greater support. Each text is collaboratively written by authors representing research and practice. Section 1 offers a practitioner's perspective on a practice in need of replacing and helps us understand the challenges, temptations, and misunderstandings that have led us to this ineffective approach. Section 2 provides a researcher's perspective on the lack of research to support the ineffective practice(s) and reviews research supporting better approaches. In Section 3, the authors representing a practitioner's perspective give detailed descriptions of how to implement these better practices. By the end of each book, you will understand both what not to do, and what to do, to improve student learning.

It takes courage to question one's own practice—to shift away from what you may have seen throughout your years in education and toward something new that you may have seen few or no colleagues use. We applaud you for demonstrating that courage and wish you the very best in your journey from this to that.

Best wishes,
—*Ellin Oliver Keene and Nell K. Duke, series editors*

# No More
# Summer-Reading Loss

**CARRIE CAHILL**

**KATHY HORVATH**

**ANNE McGILL-FRANZEN**

**RICHARD ALLINGTON**

HEINEMANN
Portsmouth, NH

**Heinemann**
361 Hanover Street
Portsmouth, NH 03801–3912
www.heinemann.com

*Offices and agents throughout the world*

The authors and publisher wish to thank those who have generously given permission to reprint borrowed material:

Figure 2–6: "Twenty Most Frequently Selected Book Titles" from "Book Selections of Economically Disadvantaged Black Elementary Students" by Lunetta M. Williams from *The Journal of Educational Research* (vol. 102, issue 1, p. 57). Copyright © 2008 by Taylor & Francis Ltd. Reprinted by permission of the Copyright Clearance Center, Inc., on behalf of Taylor & Francis Ltd.

*Acknowledgments for borrowed material continue on page x.*

**Library of Congress Cataloging-in-Publication Data**
Cahill, Carrie.
    No more summer-reading loss / Carrie Cahill, Kathy Horvath, Anne McGill-Franzen, and Richard Allington.
        pages cm – (Not this, but that)
    Includes bibliographical references.
    ISBN 978-0-325-04903-8
    1. Supplementary reading—United States. 2. Summer reading programs—United States. 3. Children—Books and reading.   I. Title.
    LB1050.58.C35 2013
    372.42—dc23                                                         2013011589

*Series editors:* Ellin Oliver Keene and Nell K. Duke
*Acquisitions editor:* Margaret LaRaia
*Production:* Vicki Kasabian
*Cover design:* Lisa A. Fowler
*Interior design:* Suzanne Heiser
*Typesetting:* Valerie Levy, Drawing Board Studios
*Manufacturing:* Veronica Bennett

Printed in the United States of America on acid-free paper
17   16   15   14   13   VP   1   2   3   4   5

# CONTENTS

# INTRODUCTION

## NELL K. DUKE

We all look forward to summer. That likely includes your own eagerness to enjoy a novel by the pool or at the beach and to catch up on a stack of work-related books you've been meaning to read. We see that reading time as a time to reenergize and expose ourselves to new worlds and new thinking. A time to grow. But for many U.S. students, reading is not part of the picture of summer. Summer is a time of little reading, literally a vacation from books.

This book is an appeal to teachers and librarians, principals, and parents to help children reimagine their summer months as a time to be immersed in books. The authors of this text are uniquely qualified to help us understand how students' summers can be different. Carrie Cahill and Kathy Horvath, well known for their instructional leadership and for promoting effective professional development, are both assistant superintendents in Chicago-area school districts. They have seen the ill effects of little reading over the summer months firsthand, and they have found many ways to make summer buzz with reading activity for the students in their districts. Anne McGill-Franzen and Dick Allington are internationally recognized experts in research on summer reading. They document both why summer reading is so important and what research suggests is effective in promoting it. Together, the authors of this text show us how to make summer reading part of the picture for all of our students.

*Credit lines continued from page iv:*

Figure 2–8: *Peabody Individual Achievement Test-Revised-Normative-Update (PIAT-R/NU)*. Copyright © 1998 NCS Pearson, Inc. Reproduced by permission. All rights reserved.

Figure 3–1: "School-Year Practices That Develop Summer Readers" adapted from *To Understand* by Ellin Oliver Keene. Copyright © 2008 by Ellin Oliver Keene. Published by Heinemann, Portsmouth, NH. Reprinted by permission.

NO MORE SUMMER-READING LOSS

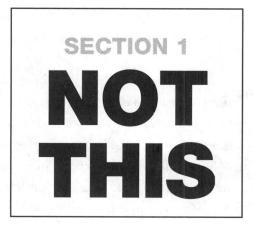

SECTION 1

NOT THIS

# I Know What You Didn't Do Last Summer

## CARRIE CAHILL and KATHY HORVATH

Imagine the last couple of weeks of school. The year is winding down. Teachers are busy packing up their rooms to prepare for the thorough cleaning of the school that happens each summer. Although the school year hasn't officially ended, we see students taking down bulletin boards and emptying their desks. It's not just an action, but a metaphor communicating that school, and everything associated with it, including reading, is over. The books are boxed up. The classroom is shut down. Summer is approaching, and it is time for fun activities (not reading). Time to celebrate!

All teachers revel in the success that their students make over the course of a year, only to release them in June to months away from the daily habit of reading and the likely regression known as summer-reading loss. Next fall in the teacher's lounge, they hear about the things that the students from last year's class can't seem to do. They think to themselves, "I know Jimmy could do that last spring.

He came so far with his thinking. He loved reading about sharks. What happened? How can I ensure this doesn't happen with my new class?"

When we began our teaching careers in education in the 1980s (Kathy, a special education teacher, and Carrie, a school social worker), we were brimming with enthusiasm for our jobs and were committed to our students' success. We were sad to see our students leave for the summer and often kept in touch by attending their baseball and softball games in June and July. When school resumed in late August, Kathy followed the usual practice, like every other teacher in her building, of reintroducing students to the habit of reading. Across the hall, throughout the building, and throughout the country, teachers spend several weeks each fall reminding students what the authentic practice of reading looks like.

All that time reteaching what students once knew but lost because they'd stopped reading over the summer! Imagine instead a classroom where students started the year bursting to talk about what they'd read, already with identities as readers and eager to read more. That invitation to imagine is an essential part of our job as teachers: We see the potential in children and use that to help them grow—not *potential* summer readers but actual summer readers. What's preventing us from turning those potential summer readers into actual ones? As you'll read in Section 2, there's over thirty years of research that explains summer-reading loss and how to stop it. Somehow, we were unaware of this information when we began teaching. If we had known then what we know now regarding the research on summer-reading loss, we would have done things differently. But we know we're not alone in this. In education, there are often valued practices that we are proud to pass on from one generation to the next, but summer-reading loss is not one of them.

Summer-reading loss is a real issue that affects student prepared-ness for the next grade level and widens the achievement gap between students of different socioeconomic backgrounds. In the crush of late spring demands, teachers may not give a second thought to the assumption that students will continue to read and discuss their reading, many without the support of parents or teachers, over the summer months. It may not occur to us that we can actually affect summer-reading habits of our students.

**How does this widening achievement gap work and what does it look like?**

see Section 2, page 19

While teachers and administrators work tirelessly to close the reading gap throughout the school year, the time between the end of one school year and the beginning of the next chips away at the reading identity and practices that students have developed during the school year. Without school support, many of our students stop reading. It is as if we are taking two steps forward during the school year and one step backward during the summer. So, to move forward, let's explore some questions that we wished we'd asked ourselves years ago.

## Do We Do Enough to Foster Independent Readers?

After participating in the routine of reading throughout the school year, it is natural to assume that students will continue to read over the summer. But we don't examine the experience through the eyes of the students. For many students, reading is seen only as a school-based activity. When the school year is over, so too is the habit of reading. These students perceive reading as an assignment or chore, rather than a pleasurable, leisure activity. Although they may have been happy readers in our classrooms, these students are not yet independent readers, readers who can, want to, and are likely to read on their own. They are still dependent on the daily literacy block schedule in which they receive instruction, support through conferences, and an opportunity to share and reflect with other students. Of course, none of those elements are present for most students in the summer. We need to explore what we can do during the school year to help students work toward independence as readers in the summer.

What happens during the summer with kids' reading isn't isolated from what happens during the school year. The lack of student reading during the summer is actually a reflection of how well we have taught them to be independent readers during the school year. In Sections 2 and 3, you'll learn how school-year instruction can build student stamina and perseverance for summer reading. Students need the tools/reading strategies and lots of practice with them to manage text independently. If we've given students enough scaffolding to support independent reading during the school year, they're more likely to read on their own during the summer. The practice of independent reading is essential for them to learn that reading is a conversation between the individual reader and the author, that encountering difficulty is a normal part of reading, and that they can push through that difficulty to uncover rich ideas about a text.

**For the research on effective reading instruction**

see Section 3, Figure 3–1, page 45

Moving students toward independence means that we help students see reading as an essential part of who they are, regardless of whether they're in school or not. During the school year, we work toward this goal by giving students time each day to read independently, write about their thinking, and share insights with peers. The school year is the time for us to establish the momentum of engagement by letting students' own preferences and interests lead them to new books and by showing them how to notice their growth as readers. We show them the path of independence through thoughtful modeling of the reading process with specific instruction and practice of the skills and strategies that help them gain a deeper understanding of what they read. These work habits, strategies, and motivation become part of who they are: self-directed, independent readers. We continue these practices until the very last day of the school year to set up an expectation that, on their own, they'll continue reading the next day and the next.

Figure 1–1 highlights some practices that when used in isolation do not develop students as independent readers. Many teachers and school

**Figure 1–1** School-Year Practices That Can Inhibit Summer Reading

| If we overemphasize this instructional practice during the school year . . . | . . . then we risk students exhibiting these attitudes and behaviors related to summer reading. |
|---|---|
| Whole-class novels | • Because of limited student choice, students don't see themselves as readers but see reading as something forced on them.<br>• Students passively accept others' interpretations of a book rather than try to make meaning for themselves. |
| Leveled text | • Students choose books or have books chosen for them because of level labels, rather than focusing on their needs and interests as readers.<br>• Students may not take risks in choosing more challenging books. |
| Fiction as the most commonly read mode | • Students don't learn how to navigate through different kinds of texts.<br>• Students get a limited sense of what reading can be, not recognizing literacy beyond books: reading online, magazines, newspapers, etc.<br>• Students get limited practice reading other genres, like informational texts, that may interest them. This may make them less able and less likely to tackle them on their own. |
| Isolated skill instruction | • Students don't see or experience the coordination of processes involved in actual reading, one that integrates reading strategies according to the needs of the reader and the demands of the text.<br>• Students don't grow as readers. |

**For the school-year practices that prepare kids for successful summer reading**

see Section 3, Figure 3–1, page 45

leaders find comfort in these practices because they give the illusion of control and coverage. We often fall into the trap of focusing our teaching on the book alone and not including explicit instruction focused on how readers get better. When a teacher focuses exclusively on a book rather than the readers in her classroom, she may be communicating to her students that reading is not essential to their identity but rather that books are a required (and perhaps unwanted) inheritance.

## Of Summer-Reading Lists and Questions: Are We Assigning Books or Inviting Students to Be Lifelong Readers?

Let's acknowledge that some of our well-intended end-of-the-year practices may actually discourage students from reading over the summer. Consider, for example, the summer-reading list that teachers thoughtfully research, craft, and refine each year, in hopes that students will keep reading and stay "busy" during the summer.

The list reflects hard work and good intention, but what does it communicate to a child? Imagine your grade school self. The last bell rings and you are heading home to begin summer vacation. You are practically out the door when the teacher hands you a booklist for summer reading. None of the titles mean anything to you, but you know the list is a command from your teacher to read at least some of them. What if all the books on the list are too hard or not interesting to you? What if it's difficult for you to get access to books over the summer? Are you motivated to start reading or anxious to put the list in a drawer and head out to play with friends? Is it any wonder why so many students don't read over the summer?

As teachers, we sometimes mistakenly hear agreement in students' silence and compliance. For the most part, students want to please us. Therefore, students will make an effort to do what is asked of them, not necessarily because they are excited about it, but because we have directed them to do so. Most summer-reading lists are created by teachers with the best of intentions. We want to ensure that students read classics or award winners, but the titles are often chosen by teams of teachers and may be their favorites but not books to which students are drawn.

**For an analysis of summer reading lists from a research perspective**

see Section 2, page 32

About eight years ago, teachers in Kathy's district developed a "sacred" reading list. This list was divided into grade-level sections, so that students could only read one small, teacher-selected group of books each summer. Each grade-level collection became something bartered for and argued over, a point of contention among teachers. But, more importantly, the act of assigning books to kids inhibited who students could become as readers, sending the message that if they didn't like and understand these three books this summer, they didn't fit.

When we say that specific book titles can only be read at a certain grade level, we make a potentially harmful assumption that all our students will be ready and eager to read the same book at the same time. Some educators defend this practice by saying that it is essential to keep certain titles fresh each year, and their students won't be as interested in reading a book for a second time. But that's only a problem when the teacher has lists of questions for each book and requires students who have already read the book to answer the same or similar questions. Rereading often leads to greater comprehension and appreciation of text. That is one reason teachers develop favorite titles in the first place. Each time teachers read the books, they create new ideas and deeper understandings. Rereading offers the chance to discover new themes and a better awareness of the nuances of text. Why not provide students with that same opportunity?

**For more on rereading as an effective summer reading practice**

see Section 3, page 49

And, while the books on these lists may be high quality, they are often too difficult or just not interesting for many students. Even if these books seem comparable in difficulty to what students read during the school year, we forget that students receive support from us as they read these more difficult books through conferring and peer discussions. At home, they are less likely to read, and if they do, will probably abandon books that are too hard for them and their negative feelings about those few summer-reading books will start to become associated with all books and reading in general. They return to school in the fall defeated by reading and more resistant to reading instruction than ever before.

What students read and whether students read should be the students' choice. Giving them choice is the first step in giving them a reason to read, and in Section 2 you'll learn the research that demonstrates why choice is the essential foundation to effective summer reading. Choice creates momentum for students to pick up one book; to read it all the way through (if they like it); to think, talk, and write about what the book means to them; and then to move on to the next book that interests them. Without choice, students wait for us to tell them what to do and they enact orders rather than read, as you can see from this student's description of summer reading.

**Why is choice so important to students' reading lives?**

see Section 2, page 21

**How can teachers support choice through specific classroom practices?**

see Section 3, page 45

Unfortunately, Jenny's experience isn't unique. Let's dig a little deeper and think not just about Jenny's attitude toward summer reading, but about the kind of reading expected in most summer-reading assignments. Recently, Jenny was assigned the novel *The Life of Pi* (Martel 2001) along with a list of questions to answer for each chapter. Because *The Life of Pi* has one hundred chapters, Jenny was given a six-page, single-spaced handout of hundreds of questions

## A Student's Perspective: "I Just Read These Books Because I Have No Choice"

*"Since I was in elementary school, every teacher sent me home with a summer-reading list and sets of questions to be completed and handed in on the first day of the new school year. These assignments counted as a grade. I read these books as quickly as I can. My older sister had the same books assigned to her and each year she gives her summaries to my older brother who passes them down to me when I need them. Each summer, I rely on her summaries to tell me what the books are about so that I can get through them as quickly as possible. I just read these books because I have no choice."*

**Jenny, a high school student**

(that's approximately one question per page of the book). The handout included questions like:

- Who is Mr. Satish Kumar and where does he work?
- What religion is Pi raised with?
- What two characters meet in this chapter (Chapter 31)?
- What is the last thing mentioned on the list of things in the lifeboat?
- Whose birthday does Pi recognize in this short chapter (Chapter 75)?

If you are familiar with *Life of Pi*, you know that there is an unexpected and disturbing ending. On Jenny's summer-reading handout, Chapter 100 listed one question that only glazed the surface of this compelling novel: "What surprising detail does Mr. Okamoto include at the end of his report?" With such questions, how could Jenny know that reading means thinking and forming your own opinions as you read? Questions that ask for minute details in a story are only meant to ensure that students are reading every word, not checking for understanding or new thinking after reading. Is it any wonder that Jenny doesn't dig into summer reading? Commanding students to read and holding them accountable with a list of questions may seem like a way to motivate students to read; however, it may contribute to a disdain for books. It's an instructional practice that achieves the opposite of our intent. These superficial questions fill Jenny's time, and her teacher's, and reflect an authoritarian–subordinate relationship of compliance. The questions and this kind of reading become a burden that Jenny all too willingly casts off the second she's no longer accountable to her teacher.

The anecdote becomes a little less abstract when we tell you that Jenny is Kathy's niece. Kathy tried to reengage Jenny in summer reading by suggesting she call her friends and divide the questions among them. Perhaps, then, she could find a book that interested her, and she could spend the rest of her time reading something enjoyable. At first speechless, Jenny then expressed fear that her teacher would call this kind of collaboration cheating. Compliance felt safer to Jenny than the risk of true reading.

In the end, students may do what is asked of them—answer questions about plot, skim through a book that's too difficult or uninteresting—or abandon ship altogether and decide that reading is not part of who they are. Both of these paths are corrosive to students' reading lives and to their sense of self: The expectations of their teachers that they will read and come to school with deep insights about what they've read is something they can't or won't meet. Ironically, when we put books into kids' hands that they don't want to read and/or can't read, we *underestimate* what they can do. We might think that an assigned book and the strategy instruction to support provide adequate scaffolding. But telling students which book to read doesn't give them a reason to read besides completion, and completion alone only motivates them to read fast, not deeply.

## Are We Making Assumptions About Children's Access to Books?

We've spent some time talking about how inhibiting students' choice of what to read makes them less inclined to read, but choice alone doesn't solve the problem of summer-reading loss. We have to realize that when we end the school year, we are also ending many students' access to books. Children from low-socioeconomic families often have fewer printed materials, such as newspapers, magazines, and books at home. Although we know access is an issue, do we see workable solutions? The absence of print in children's home environment adds to the

**For ideas on how to get more books into students' hands**

see Section 3, page 49

perception that reading is solely a school activity. Without ensuring access to books, we may be setting students up for failure before the new school year begins.

A school district in a lower-socioeconomic suburb south of Chicago has no school libraries. In fact, there is no community library either. The neighboring town does not allow students from that community to check out books because they are not residents. Public libraries in middle-class communities often host summer programs that build in reading incentives or socialization around books, but many children can't get to or use those libraries. They may bring in authors and other speakers to connect with student interests. When students from low-socioeconomic families have no access to the community libraries, they are missing out on these opportunities as well. Bookmobile programs, which have been an effective way of providing access to underserved communities, have diminished due to lack of funding (Andrews 2012). This lack of access describes not only urban but rural settings, where

**What are the specific consequences of no summer reading?**

see Section 2, page 17

resources like libraries and computer access to online materials can be sparse (Malhoit 2005). As you'll find out in Section 2, the consequences for this lack of access are real for our students, resulting in lower academic achievement than their peers who do have access.

## Why Is It So Difficult for Parents to Get Their Children to Read?

**For effective ways to get parents involved**

see Section 3, page 56

Teachers communicate the importance of reading to parents and most parents want to be our partners in this work, but they may not be sure how to help. Some parents request work from their child's teacher as a desperate attempt at keeping their child connected to learning, even if it's just busywork. Sending home worksheets and practice pages is probably one of the best ways to destroy any chance that students will pick up a book over the summer. Parents often feel that they need to have an expectation from the school to keep their children learning over the summer, and they gratefully point to the summer-reading list provided by teachers saying, "Your teacher says that you have to read these books." What they may not realize, however, is that their enforcement of reading the books on the list may make their children more resistant to authentic reading.

Last July, when Carrie was getting her monthly haircut, Kim, Carrie's hairdresser, brought up the topic of summer reading. Because of her relationship with Carrie and the fact that Carrie is an educator, Kim felt comfortable expressing her frustration at trying to get her boys, ages seven and ten, to read. She told Carrie about the structures she'd put in place to ensure summer reading: twenty minutes a day mandatory reading time, a selection of books at home, and regular library visits so that Monty and Mason could choose books they want to read. She told the boys that they must read to prepare for the coming school year, but every day was a struggle. Kim was concerned that her children dislike reading so much that she had to force them to read. Reading time had become stressful for her because her children saw it as a punishment. Kim knew that reading is the key to being successful in school. She was willing and ready to try anything, but needed some suggestions. How many parents share her frustration? Teachers can help (and we'll show you how in Section 3).

## Why Aren't Summer School Programs Filling the Gap?

Assigning struggling readers to summer school is a common practice in school districts. The idea of continuing academics over the summer seems like a sensible solution. But, sadly, summer school is often seen as a punishment; students are often assigned to summer school because they haven't reached a certain level of achievement during the school year. Even with the best intentions, many summer school programs do not schedule enough time for authentic reading, especially since some time is needed for art and physical activity. Students' participation in summer school is often filled with less noble activities: the copy machine in many schools burns hot copying useless worksheets and puzzles when students could be having meaningful reading experiences. Years of observing summer school has taught us that the design of a summer school program is crucial in addressing summer-reading loss. If summer school is not designed in a thoughtful, informed manner, it can be just another stretch of programs and worksheets that do nothing to promote better reading habits. As a result, students may start off the new school year even more disengaged from reading.

Here's one student's perspective on a common summer school activity—timed oral reading—and there are many more summer school activities that fit Tony's description of "not real reading."

## A Student's Perspective: "This Isn't Real Reading"

*"Oh, this isn't real reading. I am just practicing saying lots of sentences quickly. When I read, I have a real book in my hands."*

**Tony, a third-grade student**

Schools are easily seduced into spending money on "not real reading." Summer school and reading remediation funds go to packages and computer programs that promise quick results and mindless implementation. The instruction in these programs is often structured on models of authority and submission fostering passive, compliant children rather than independent thinkers, children who succeed and grow.

We acknowledge here that many of the practices teachers believe encourage summer reading actually have the opposite effect. The eight- to twelve-week summer break is often a real obstacle to student learning, particularly students from lower-socioeconomic communities. Teachers and school leaders struggle to invent solutions, but the good news is that we already have insights about what to do. Let's read what thirty years of research tell us about effective summer-reading practices.

# WHY NOT? WHAT WORKS?

## Children Will Read During the Summer If We Provide Access, Choice, and Support

ANNE McGILL-FRANZEN and RICHARD ALLINGTON

Sometimes rather than an expectation, our summer-reading practice is a hope: We hope children will read over the summer, but we accept that they often don't. We resign ourselves to this because we believe that there's not much else we can do to help, but there is. In this section, we'll share the research that explains not only why summer reading is a necessary practice but also how a meaningful summer-reading program should be structured to include student choice, access to diverse and interesting books that children want to read, and supports to ensure children keep reading.

First, let's assess the value of summer reading. Over thirty years ago, a research study demonstrated that the *only* summer activity related to improving reading achievement is summer reading (Heyns 1978). So we've known (and known it for a long time) that summer reading has value, but what happens when kids don't read? By comparing students' spring and fall test scores, Heyns, along with researchers Entwisle, Alexander, and Olson (1997), identified "summer setback"—the phenomenon of declining academic achievement during summer recess. This loss in reading often takes teachers by surprise in the fall of each school year when students are not performing at the same level as in the spring of the previous year. But just reading a few books over the summer can stem the loss in reading achievement as Kim (2004) demonstrated in his analysis of a school district-sponsored voluntary summer-reading program for sixth-grade students. In this study the effects of reading four or five books over the summer months was "potentially large enough to prevent a decline in reading achievement scores from spring to the fall" (Kim 2004, 169). It's a given. Summer reading is essential to maintaining all students' school-year academic success.

## Why Some Children Read During the Summer and Some Don't

Summer means some kids are reading and some are not. Summer affects students differently, depending on whether or not they live in low-socioeconomic communities or attend low-socioeconomic schools. All students *should* read during the summer, but children without any books *can't* read. Some parents plan summers filled with enrichment activities and take trips to the local library or bookstore to provide their children with access to books; families of other children may not have the resources to buy books or make trips to the library. We'll explore the reasons why children who have access to books don't read, but first let's talk about what access to books (or lack of access) during the summer means for student achievement. Figure 2–1 illustrates why family income may predict reading achievement. Income enables families to provide resources, like books in the home, and these resources in turn support children's literacy development and educational achievement. Higher levels of educational attainment and schooling are related to higher income, and these patterns may be repeated across generations.

**Figure 2–1  An Income-Achievement Feedback Mechanism**

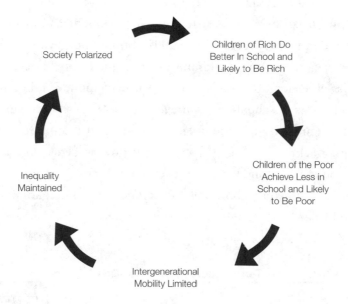

Society Polarized

Children of Rich Do Better In School and Likely to Be Rich

Children of the Poor Achieve Less in School and Likely to Be Poor

Inequality Maintained

Intergenerational Mobility Limited

Note: Educational achievement predicts income, income enables parents to buy cognitive resources like books, and cognitive resources predict educational achievement (Reardon 2011).

As if we didn't know it, research demonstrates that schools can serve their purpose of social equity. When school is in session, students from low-socioeconomic families typically learn at the same rate as their financially better-off peers (Alexander, Entwisle, and Olson 2007). But there's a structural problem that's out of individual teachers' hands. When school is not in session, the learning resources of the school are turned off—like a faucet. Typically, students from low-socioeconomic communities lose two months of reading achievement during the summer months and students from more advantaged communities gain a month during the summer (Cooper et al. 1996). In a study tracking students' achievement each spring and summer from school entry through the fifth grade, the overall gap in achievement grew wider with each year of school, ultimately culminating in a lag of several years (Entwisle, Alexander, and Olson 1997). Of course, the gap doesn't stop growing at grade 6 but continues to widen through middle school, resulting in an even greater reading achievement gap at ninth grade (Alexander, Entwisle, and Olson 2007). Simply put, even when schools in low-socioeconomic communities are equally effective as those in middle-class neighborhoods and low-socioeconomic children hold their own in terms of school-year achievement, the two-month summer loss in achievement would accumulate over time and account for most of the rich/poor achievement gap, a gap that is now twice as large as the gap between minority and white achievement (Duncan and Murnane 2011). Figure 2–2 illustrates how small differences at kindergarten add up to several years by the beginning of sixth grade.

**Figure 2–2   Long-Term Effects of Summer-Reading Loss**

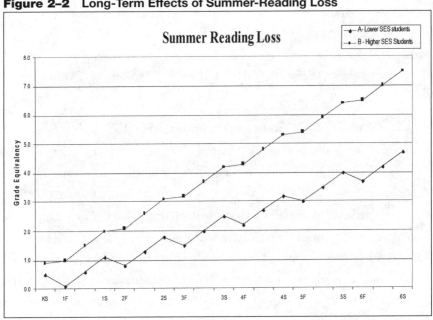

Note: Zigzag pattern illustrates summer setback with spring and fall test scores. Scores increase in the spring and decline or "fall back" in the fall, demonstrating summer-reading loss from first through sixth grade. The summer-reading gap increases over the grades (Cooper et al. 1996; Entwisle, Alexander, and Olson 1997).

So it's clear that summer reading requires support, but adding to the sense of urgency is the awareness that the gap may be widening as many families' resources dwindle and they are less able to invest financially in extras for their children. In fact, parental income is now nearly as strong a predictor of achievement as parental education and a more powerful predictor of achievement than race (Reardon 2011). While this calcification of class may seem grim, it's not one that we should passively resign ourselves to. There are simple, research-proven steps that any classroom teacher can take to ensure summer reading happens for all students, regardless of income.

## How Limited Access to Books Affects Summer Reading

Let's first take a minute to consider the practice of providing summer-reading lists, something most schools typically do. Although there's no research to support the practice of providing parents with suggested reading lists, it's not necessarily a bad idea. After all, as adults, we choose what to read based on the recommendations of trusted resources like friends, book reviews, Amazon ratings. But gathering the books on a list is a task that some parents may not have the resources to enact, either by purchasing the recommended books or even borrowing them from the public library, due to relatively limited library resources in low-socioeconomic neighborhoods (Bradley et al. 2001; Constantino 2005; Neuman and Celano 2001; Smith, Constantino, and Krashen 1997). One can see how a booklist fosters a deficit model of what low-socioeconomic children don't have, unlike their more affluent peers. Let's put books in kids' hands, not lists.

Putting books in children's hands creates a different relationship and different effects. Researchers Halle, Kurtz-Costes, and Mahoney (1997) examined parental behaviors and attitudes among a group of African American parents

> **For ideas on how to get books in children's hands**
>
> see Section 3, page 49

living in a low-socioeconomic urban community. The only behavioral or environmental measure that correlated with reading achievement was the number of books in the home. They concluded that providing poor children with books may be the most critical thing a school can do: "Because many of these families cannot afford to purchase children's books, it becomes all the more important to make [books] . . . easily and readily available within disadvantaged communities" (535).

In another study of families that identified both socioeconomic status and race (Fryer and Levitt 2002), more affluent homes had two to three times as many books as less affluent homes and this gap in book ownership accurately predicted kindergarten and first-grade reading achievement. Because being a minority and being poor unfortunately often overlap in our country, these statistics accounted for the entire reading gap between black and white students and most of the gap between Hispanic and white students.

In fact, what educators view as "home support" for literacy development is inextricably bound to issues of access to books. Dickinson and DeTemple (1998) found in a study of eighty-three families that home support (defined by the number of books in the home, library visits, reading to the child, other print resources) for literacy when children were in preschool was positively correlated with literacy achievement in grade 1. Home support was also a significant predictor of story comprehension and performance on vocabulary in kindergarten. In other words, children who arrive at school from homes where many books have been available are the students who do well in school, often despite other factors such as lower socioeconomic status or parental education levels.

Access to books is important in different countries as well. In a study of 70,000 families in twenty-seven nations, Evans and colleagues (2010) found the effect of home access to books was about the same as parental education, twice as large as father's occupation, and stronger than family socioeconomic status. Children who grew up in homes where there were many books likely attended an additional three years of schooling compared to children from homes where there were few books available.

Based on these international data we can see the "feedback mechanism" at work: cognitive resources, like books in the home, support educational achievement; educational achievement means more schooling and access to higher earnings; and higher earnings enable investment in the next generation for families of parents who have succeeded in school.

The point we seek to make here is simple: Some kids come from homes and communities where books are accessible but too many of our lowest-achieving students come from homes and communities where few books are present. To disrupt this feedback cycle of low achievement in school that mires these children and their future families in poverty, we need to provide resources that count—books for out-of-school summer reading.

## Why Student Choice Is So Important

It's clear that providing all children with access to books is a necessity, but who chooses the books that the children read? The answer, research tells us, should be the children. Support for student choice derives from a number of research studies. Guthrie and Humenick (2004), for example, evaluated twenty-two studies designed to improve reading outcomes and found just four factors that explained almost all of the variance in motivation and reading achievement. See Figure 2–3.

The two largest contributions to reading achievement were *access to interesting books* and *student choice of the books* they would read. Both factors moved reading achievement ahead more than a full standard deviation (effect size [ES] $\geq$ 1.0), which would move a student from the 16th to greater than the 50th percentile on standardized tests of reading comprehension.

Similarly, in an analysis of the research on book distribution projects, such as Reading Is Fundamental (RIF), Lindsay (2013) noted that

> **For ideas on how to create your own book distribution project**
>
> see Section 3, page 51

**Figure 2–3**  Motivational Classroom Practices for Increasing Reading Achievement

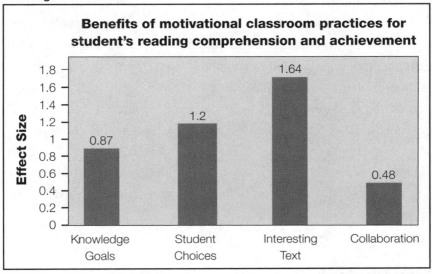

(Guthrie and Humenick 2004, 333)

studies that simply improved children's access to interesting books without adding any additional support had powerful effects in fostering reading development and motivation to read (ES = 0.44). Book distribution projects like Reading Is Fundamental (RIF) that *give* books to children, rather than simply *lend* books to children, cause improved reading outcomes. By synthesizing the results of more than one hundred studies that met criteria for scientific rigor, Lindsay was able to identify the following positive behavioral outcomes of book-giveaway programs: improved attitudes, motivation, reading volume, and emergent literacy and reading performance (Lindsay 2013; see Figure 2–4). However, Lindsay also noted that studies in which children were given choices of reading material showed substantially larger effects on reading achievement than did studies where children had no such choice. When children were given the opportunity to choose books,

**Figure 2–4**  Positive Student Behaviors Due to Free Book Programs

| Positive Behavior | Effect Sizes | Which Means Increased Percentile Scores from Average to . . . |
|---|---|---|
| Attitude toward reading | +0.38 | 65th percentile |
| Motivation to read | +0.97 | 83rd percentile |
| Reading behavior (such as how much and how often children read) | +0.56 | 71st percentile |
| Language abilities | +0.14 | 56th percentile |
| Emergent literacy skills | +0.44 | 67th percentile |
| Reading performance | +0.43 | 66th percentile |
| Writing performance | +0.25 | 60th percentile |

(Lindsay 2013, 31)

reading gains were almost double those of children whose books were selected by someone else (Lindsay 2013). The number and quality of materials, parent or teacher guidance and encouragement, and the inclusion of other literacy activities increased the effectiveness of book distribution projects (Lindsay 2013).

If we put books in children's hands, positive reading behaviors follow. This one act lays a strong foundation for summer reading. But when we say "put books in children's hands," we don't just mean any book and we don't mean books that we choose for them.

It's clear that providing all children with access to books is a necessity, but who chooses what children read? Earlier, we said that despite having access to books many children still choose not to read over the summer. They may choose not to read because they don't have a choice of what to read. Remember, in Lindsay's meta-analysis of book giveaway programs, when children were given the opportunity to choose books, reading gains were twice those of children whose books were selected by someone else (Lindsay 2013).

And this makes sense, right? "Choice" is not an abstract concept, but reflects our sense of agency in the world. Not just choosing *whether* to read, but choosing *what* they will read empowers students: life—and reading in particular—is not something thrust upon them. Dav Pilkey, author of the extremely popular Captain Underpants series, mused on the importance of choice in kids' lives when he said: "What if all of your reading material was selected by, or restricted by people who believed that they knew what was best for you. Wouldn't that be awful? Wouldn't you resent it? And isn't it possible that you might begin to associate books with bad things like drudgery and subjugation?" (Pilkey 2011, 28).

> **For ideas on how to ensure that reading doesn't just happen in one class, but across grade levels**
>
> see Section 3

If students are going to read during the summer, then a system that depends on the teacher or parent as enforcer of "drudgery and subjugation" just won't work. We want students to recognize that reading is one of many positive life choices they can make. To test the value of access combined with choice, we organized book fairs of 400 to 600 titles from which students selected twelve to fifteen free books to read each summer for three consecutive summers (Allington et al. 2010). The students in the study were randomly selected from two grade levels (beginning with end of year first- and second-grade students) in seventeen high-poverty schools located in two southeastern school districts—one urban and the other a rural, agricultural community. Most of the participating students were from low-socioeconomic families eligible for free or reduced-price meals. Almost all of the participants (90%) were members of an ethnic minority, mostly African American, with some Haitian and some Central and Latin American immigrant children.

At the end of our study we found that the children who had participated in the book fairs and received free, self-selected books for summer reading significantly improved reading achievement on high-stakes state tests when compared to their peers in the control group who received no summer books. The ES on reading achievement was 0.14 for the full sample and 0.21 for the poorest children, those eligible for free lunch in each group. By comparing our results with other more costly and intrusive interventions, we can make the practical significance of the book fair study more transparent and highlight the importance of providing access to books and student choice in summer-reading programs.

To put our overall effect size in perspective, it is the same result that can be expected from having students participate in three years of summer school (Cooper et al. 2000). The Cooper et al. meta-analysis of fifty-four summer school studies demonstrated just that—summer school participation had an ES of 0.14, the same effect as providing poor students free books for three consecutive summers, as we did in our study. Even more surprising, our book fair achieved the same or better result than participation in schoolwide reform efforts, which Borman and colleagues (2003) calculated to have an ES between 0.09 and 0.14. The Coalition for Evidence-Based Policy (2011) described the results of our project another way: The annual book fair led to "an increase in students' reading achievement by 35–40% of a grade level three years after random assignment" to the project at a total "3-year cost of $175–$225 per student" (3), far less than many prepackaged reading intervention programs. The coalition examined the average annual gain in reading achievement on seven nationally normed assessments (Bloom et al. 2008) and on that basis, calculated the benefit of our book fair project on students' performance.

## Which Books Do Children Want to Read?

A key component of our study was giving students choice from a collection of books we thought they'd want to read. *Choice* didn't just mean dropping children off at the public library but *supported* choice based on what we know about children, their approximate reading levels, and their preferences. Which books do children want to read? Here are some key findings from our research and the work of others.

**Figure 2–5** Which Books Do Students Want to Read?

| Books Students Want to Read |
| --- |
| • Series books popular with different ages |
| • Pop culture and sports biographies |
| • Funny books |
| • Books with arresting visual features |
| • Nonfiction about topics that resonate with boys and girls |
| • Graphic novels |

**We can't assume that boys and girls will choose books based on gender stereotypes.** What books do students want to read? Canadian researchers Chapman et al. (2007) studied first graders' book selections in tasks that presented both narrative and informational books on similar topics and found no preferences for either storybooks or informational books based on the children's gender. In other words, boys and girls were likely to choose both types of books, and in fact, boys in this study—working-class Canadian boys—were more likely to select storybooks than informational books for their own personal reading, a finding that challenges the perception that boys typically prefer nonfiction. *Froggy Goes to Bed* (London 2000) and *Life Cycle of a Frog* (Royston 2000) are examples of the kinds of books that the researchers presented to children to get a sense of their preferences. Besides asking children to choose books, the researchers interviewed them about why they selected particular books. These first graders were more likely to cite awards, humor, visual interest, and topics as features that attracted them, rather than the genre per se. When the researchers asked the children which books most other boys or girls would pick for their reading, as opposed to the children's personal reading preferences, the responses were different and gendered. In other words, the children, as part of our culture that communicates images and notions of traditional masculinity and femininity, subscribed wholeheartedly to the stereotypes of what most boys read ("gross things") or what most girls read ([not] "about scary spiders"). When these first graders chose books for other boys and girls, they chose the informational books for boys and the storybooks for girls, "even though their perceptions (especially boys') were not consistent with their own interests" (7). The authors noted the limitations of gender stereotyping in choosing books for children because "not all children experience literacy in the same way" (7), and boys and girls both reap the benefits of reading narrative *and* informational texts.

**Visual features, humor, interesting topics, are cited as reasons to choose a book more often than genre or even recommendations by friends.** Earlier work by Mohr (2003, 2006), again with first graders, also found that children held similar beliefs about the topics that they thought boys versus girls would like to read, although in her study, both boys and girls selected the nonfiction books—the exact same three nonfiction books. Mohr's study may not be comparable to Chapman et al.'s study (2007), or to other research reviewed in this section, because she provided only nine books from which children could select a single book to own. Other studies have provided many more books from which to choose, ranging from forty to over four hundred. The smaller selection probably limits inferences that we might like to make about young children's reading preferences. Nonetheless, the first graders in this study selected books based on the same features identified in other studies (Chapman et al. 2007, for example). Children here as elsewhere gravitated toward visual features, humor, and interesting topics rather than genre or even recommendations by friends, and they wanted to share their book with family. The book overwhelmingly selected by boys—*Animals Nobody Loves* (Simon 2001)—also happened to be the most challenging, but boys seemed unfazed by the difficulty. Besides *Animals Nobody Loves* (Simon 2001), students selected the rhyming book, *There's a Zoo in Room 22* (Sierra 2000), and the humorous *What Moms Can't Do* (Wood 2000). The results of this study challenged not only assumptions about the primacy of narrative and gender stereotypes in children's reading preferences but also the belief that children prefer books that mirror their own ethnicity or linguistic heritage. In this study of approximately 200 students, many of them Hispanic, that clearly was not the case: "Although many educators argue that students need exposure to multicultural books, this research suggests that first graders may be less interested in such stories and may not yet prefer multicultural texts as 'windows and mirrors' of the world around them" (Mohr 2003, 173).

On the other hand, there just are not that many books with nonwhite Latino children as central characters, according to a recent news story (Rich 2012). Even though Hispanic children represent about 25 percent of the school-aged population, fewer than 3 percent of books reviewed by the Cooperative Children's Book Center in 2011 were about Latinos or written by Latinos, a percentage that the University of Wisconsin–based center claimed has not changed in the past ten years, and only two of the most popular series books presented a prominent Latino character. An eight-year-old interviewed by the author succinctly made the same point: "I see a lot of people that don't have a lot of color" (Rich 2012, 1).

We can't say for certain why students don't choose multicultural books more often. In another recent study Williams (2008) examined the reading preferences of approximately 300 eight- to twelve-year-old African American students who were third-year participants in a larger summer book distribution project. Like Mohr (2003, 2006), she found that students were unlikely to select multicultural literature that reflected their cultural heritage. Rather, these elementary students selected books based on familiarity and pop culture cache. Girls as well as boys selected nonfiction. Particularly popular were (unauthorized) biographies of celebrities—singers, TV and movie stars, and professional sports icons—followed by series books that sounded naughty (Captain Underpants) or had particular resonance for children within that age range (Harry Potter, Junie B. Jones, or Goosebumps). To illustrate this point, in Figure 2–6 we reproduce a table from Williams (2008, 57), which lists in rank order the top twenty titles that students selected from approximately 400 books. In some cases students identified book features, such as the cover, illustrations, or format ("flip-o-rama") as attracting them; in other cases, they identified themselves as someone who reads that series book ("I want this Junie B. Jones book"; 55) or who knows a lot about a celebrity ("She plays Lizzie McGuire and that's my favorite show"; 55). On occasion, students selected a book because the teacher recommended it or read it aloud, but peers frequently influenced book selection during the book distribution process. In the few cases where students selected culturally relevant books, such as *Pink and Say* or *Ruby Bridges*, they said their teachers had read them during Black History month.

Analysis of these eight- to twelve-year-olds' preferences over the three years of our summer book fair project, of which Williams' (2008) study is a part, suggested that although particular titles changed, the topics and genres did not (Allington et al. 2010). Nonfiction unauthorized biographies, series books, and other books that tapped into what was familiar and relevant in students' lives maintained popularity. The number one choice of primarily African American students across seventeen schools, three grade levels, and two districts (one urban, one rural) the first year was *Superman's First Flight*, the second year, *The Unauthorized Biography of Brittany Spears*, the third, *Hangin' with Lil' Romeo*. The most popular series was Captain Underpants among both boys and girls—for its humor.

**Figure 2–6**  Twenty Most Frequently Selected Book Titles

*Pop People: Destiny's Child* (Glass 2001)

*Pop People: Lil' Romeo* (Morreale 2003)

*Hangin' with Hilary Duff* (Scholastic 2003)

*Hangin' with Lil' Romeo* (Walsh 2002)

*Scary Creatures: Big Cats* (Clark, Riley, and Bergen 2003)

*Ghostville Elementary: New Ghoul in School* (Jones and Dadey 2003)

*Hey Lil' D: It's All in the Name* (Lanier, Goodyear, and Preller 2003)

*Hey Lil' D: Take the Court* (Lanier, Goodyear, and Grover 2003)

*What Did I Do to Deserve a Sister Like You?* (Medearis 2002)

*Junie B. First Grader: Boss of Lunch* (Park 2003)

*Captain Underpants and the Invasion of the Incredibly Naughty Cafeteria Ladies* (Pilkey 1999)

*The Captain Underpants Extra-Crunchy Book O' Fun* (Pilkey 2001)

*The All New Captain Underpants Extra-Crunchy Book O' Fun #2* (Pilkey 2002)

*Captain Underpants and the Big, Bad Battle of the Bionic Booger Boy, Part 1* (Pilkey 2003)

*Captain Underpants and the Big, Bad Battle of the Bionic Booger Boy, Part 2* (Pilkey 2003)

*The Adventures of Super Diaper Baby* (Pilkey, Beard, and Hutchins 2002)

*Meet the Stars of Professional Wrestling* (Preller 2000)

*Harry Potter and the Goblet of Fire* (Rowling 2002)

*How to Draw Spiderman* (Scholastic 2004)

*Goosebumps: Haunted Mask II* (Stine 2004)

(Williams 2008, 57)

**Across grade levels, the most popular books are series books.**
Clearly, publishers have struck gold with series books—both narrative
and informational. The annual report by Renaissance Learning, *What
Children Are Reading: The Book Reading Habits of Students in American
Schools* (November 2012), ranked the popularity of books read by over
seven million students in 25,000 schools, grades 1–12 based on Accel-
erated Reader data on book selection. Readers of all ages love following the characters and cross-book story lines of series books (McGill-
Franzen 2009). The formulaic plots and familiar settings may provide
a kind of comfort to young readers, helping them navigate ever longer
chapter books with increasingly sophisticated language and narrative
elements. As students move through the series, they not only develop
skills and build fluency but also begin to think of themselves as readers belonging to a peer group that reads—they know the characters by
name, they anticipate plot twists, they judge the outcomes—just like
participants in adult book clubs—and their anticipation of the next
book in the series and eagerness to discuss it with their peers maintains
their reading momentum. You might ask, what are the current favored
series books, or most popular books in general, that students *choose* to
read at different grade levels? See Figure 2–7.

**As students mature, so do their reading choices.** As students
move into the middle grades, they start to choose books that are more
likely to be challenged for mature content—the Crank trilogy by Ellen Hopkins, the Gossip Girl series by Cecily von Ziegesar, Stephenie
Meyer's Twilight series, and James Patterson's Maximum Ride. Obvi-
ously, student preferences may collide with parental or school norms
about appropriate content or literary merit. At this point, you might
ask, what *should* kids read?

You'll probably be or have been in a situation where you've worried
about what to allow. We can't navigate the difficulty of the specifics for
you, but can only present you with perspectives that might help you

**Figure 2–7**  **Most Popular Series Books for Different Grade Levels**

| What are the most popular series books at different grade levels? | |
|---|---|
| First grade | Biscuit by Alyssa Satin Capucilli <br> Fly Guy by Ted Arnold <br> Books by Dr. Seuss[1] <br> Black Lagoon by Mike Thaler <br> Henry and Mudge by Cynthia Rylant |
| Second grade | Books by Dr. Seuss[1] <br> If You Give a . . . by Laura Numeroff <br> Magic Tree House by Mary Pope Osborne <br> Amelia Bedelia by Peggy Parish |
| Third grade | Diary of a Wimpy Kid[2] by Jeff Kinney <br> Captain Underpants by Dav Pilkey <br> Percy Jackson and the Olympians series by Rick Riordan <br> Books by Judy Blume[1] <br> Babymouse series by Jenifer L. Holm <br> Bone by Jeff Smith |
| Fourth grade | Babymouse series by Jenifer L. Holm <br> Bone by Jeff Smith <br> Diary of a Wimpy Kid[2] by Jeff Kinney <br> Captain Underpants by Dav Pilkey <br> Percy Jackson and the Olympians series by Rick Riordan <br> Harry Potter by J. K. Rowling <br> Dork Diaries by Rachel Rene Russell |

| What are the most popular series books at different grade levels? | |
|---|---|
| Fifth grade | Babymouse series by Jenifer L. Holm |
| | Bone by Jeff Smith |
| | Diary of a Wimpy Kid[2] by Jeff Kinney |
| | Captain Underpants by Dav Pilkey |
| | Percy Jackson and the Olympians series by Rick Riordan |
| | Series of Unfortunate Events by Lemony Snicket (pen name of Daniel Handler) |
| Sixth grade | Babymouse series by Jenifer L. Holm |
| | Bone by Jeff Smith |
| | Diary of a Wimpy Kid[2] by Jeff Kinney |
| | Captain Underpants by Dav Pilkey |
| | Percy Jackson and the Olympians series by Rick Riordan |
| | Series of Unfortunate Events by Lemony Snicket (pen name of Daniel Handler) |
| | Hunger Games by Suzanne Collins |

(Renaissance Learning 2012)

1. Although these books are not series books, the author's choice of similar structure and characters make them associated with series books by children.

2. Diary of a Wimpy Kid was the number one choice in grades 3–5.

make your decision. Dan Gutman (2012), author of My Weird School series, answered the question, "What should kids read?" with

> Whatever they want. Just like some people like to eat meat, and others prefer vegetables, there are different kinds of readers. Some people love to get lost in a beautifully written word picture with flowery, formal sentences. Some people will only read nonfiction, or graphic novels. (v)

If readers discover that reading is *not* a chore, "they may be more willing to try other authors and other styles of writing" (v). Jeff Kinney, author of the wildly popular Diary of a Wimpy Kid series, is testimony to the truth of Gutman's statement. Kinney describes following his own path in reading: first, "gobbling up" the Dr. Seuss books before moving on to the poetry of Shel Silverstein because it was the most compelling choice for that time in his life: "Silverstein shared characteristics that spoke to me at that age; a clean line and a wicked sense of humor" (2012, 1).

Avid adult readers, interviewed for an ethnography of reading by Canadian librarian Catherine Ross and her colleagues (2005), reported a similar maturing of literary tastes. Involvement with particular characters, authors, and themes changed over the years for these committed readers as they themselves changed. As they became more proficient readers, they "graduated" to increasingly more literate and challenging texts, but, at each phase, different authors, different series "spoke to them" and were important in their developing sense of themselves as readers and as people who read (Ross et al. 2005). Ross and her colleagues found that the avid adult readers in this study did not see reading as a solitary activity, but instead "a social activity, embedded in the social relations of childhood" (226). These adult readers remembered reading a particular series books "because everyone else was reading them!" (224). At particular points in time, different series books had cachet—traded like baseball cards or hoarded like something precious. Although Ross and colleagues' study involved adult readers retrospectively examining their reading habits, Dyson (2003) observed firsthand that children use shared references to media and books to create new identities for themselves as well.

## Children Create Their Identity from Shared References to Media and Books

Children appropriate characters from media and books (Dyson 2003); they take up themes, such as heroism, supernatural powers, and good guys versus bad guys; and they enact text features, like "summarizing claims" ["he saved the world!"]. Children's writing and drawing reflect orthographic conventions found in books, comics, and media, such as stylized print, jagged lines, arrows, drawings; and what Dyson called "embedded ideologies of gender, physical power and love" and "embedded conceptual material" representing children's personal knowledge of animals, habitats, or sports gleaned from media and books (113). Because students seek and create identities based in part on the company they keep in books, edgy characters and glamorous (or risky) settings appeal to middle-grade boys and girls alike. One young girl, quoted by Pierce (2007) claimed that she cannot put Gossip Girl books down—"It has the right amount of sex, drugs, bad language and parties" (76). The Gossip Girl series has appeal across the middle grades, the books are written at a level between fourth and sixth grade. Young people may be drawn to these series because the books are a source of information about sexuality and other issues relevant to their lives. One can certainly argue about the value of the information provided on these topics, but the relevance of the topic is what engages them and keeps them reading. We have to think about balancing our different goals for children, so instead of saying kids can't read Gossip Girl, perhaps we need to make sure they have access to other information.

## Children Need Lots of Choice: Diverse Topics, Diverse Genres, and Diverse Reading Levels

It is not just the total number of books that is important. Nor is it simply choice. To maximize the potential of voluntary summer reading, the corpus of books from which students choose must itself be diverse enough to accommodate a wide range of achievement levels as well as interests. What's the right number of book choices to provide per student? As many as forty books per Lexile group may not be enough (Vitiello 2008). In his study, for example, Vitiello directed each third- and fourth-grade participant to a single bin of approximately forty books from which they could select eight summer-reading choices.

Given the range of reading levels typically found at any grade level (see Figure 2–8; Hargis 2006) and potential interests, the number and range of books provided in this study appears woefully inadequate. Perhaps those who read fewer than four or none would have read more if they had had more from which to choose. However, this doesn't mean that you should lose hope if you can only offer students a smaller number of choices when you begin this work in your own classroom, but be aware of what that smaller choice means. In Vitiello's study, students who read more than four books had an average Lexile gain of 80 points, while students who read fewer than four books lost reading achievement during the summer and those who read none of their books or only one book over the summer lost 50 Lexile points in reading achievement. As adult readers, we know that we sometimes start and don't finish books, so our summer-reading selection process for children should build in the assumption that they'll read fewer books than they select.

## Why Summer Reading Needs to Happen *Every* Summer

A summer-reading program is only truly effective if it happens every summer for every student. As part of a series of studies using similar methodology as in our study, Kim (2006) reported that a single-year summer book distribution program had only "marginally significant" effects on fall reading achievement. This marginally significant outcome may be the result of expecting too much from too little—a single summer project—and the vagaries of educational measurement over a very short period of time. That is, even if providing books for summer reading improved student reading achievement as much as attending school for three months, measuring that effect is difficult on most group achievement tests due to the large standard error of measurement associated with virtually all group reading assessments. However, it seems reasonable to extrapolate that because summer-reading

**Figure 2–8**   Range of Reading Levels in K–8

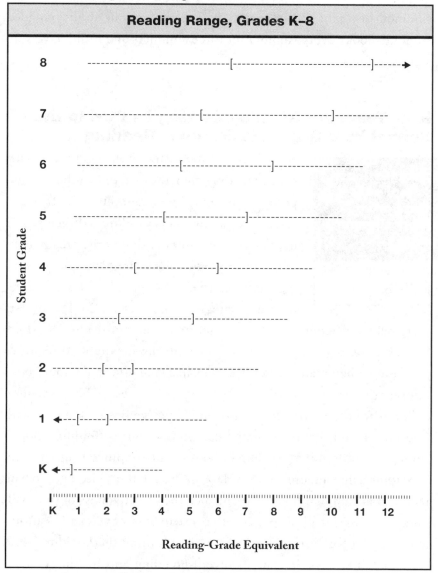

Note: The space between brackets at each grade indicates the reading level of the middle half of the class. At the first, second, and third grades, the range extends below the first-grade reading level into reading-readiness levels. In kindergarten, almost a quarter of the students can read above the first-grade level. The data used to prepare this graph were extracted from the 1998 Normative Update for the Peabody Individual Achievement Test-Revised (Markwardt 1998; Hargis 2006, 395).

Children Will Read During the Summer If We Provide Access, Choice, and Support   **37** loss happens each summer, summer reading needs to happen every summer, just as it did in our study. Remember, our study provided students books every summer for three summers and it did have substantial effects!

## How Teaching Reading Strategies During the School Year Supports Summer Reading

**For suggestions of school-year instruction to support summer reading**

see Section 3, page 45

If students are interested in the content of what they're reading, then they have an authentic purpose—to find out more about the topic. Teachers can give them the tools to address difficulty and deepen their comprehension as they read books of interest by providing strategy instruction during the school year. Research on the effectiveness of strategies (Duke et al. 2011) suggests that such instruction may be an important summer-reading scaffold. Strategies help students persevere despite the inevitable difficulties presented when reading. For example, in a single-year summer books intervention study (White and Kim 2008), the researchers provided children from low-socioeconomic families in grades 3, 4, and 5 with free books, and oral reading and comprehension scaffolding prior to summer. Children in this summer books study improved significantly in reading achievement compared to children in the control group who received no summer books. To enhance the effectiveness of their voluntary summer-reading project, the researchers developed scaffolding procedures that teachers implemented during the last three days of school. Teachers' lessons involved modeling and making explicit the five comprehension strategies (119)—rereading, predicting, questioning, making connections, and summarizing—that students could use independently during the summer and providing opportunities for oral reading practice of 100-word passages. Every week for eight weeks during the summer students received a book matched to their reading levels and interests in the mail along with a postcard survey.

Because teachers won't be monitoring students during the summer for stamina and perseverance, we want to make sure we give them the tools to work through struggles on their own. We can let them know that it's okay to abandon some books, but also make sure they know that encountering difficulty in a book doesn't always mean abandoning it. Of course, if the content is interesting to students and they are reading for their own purposes, they are more likely to engage with the book, read strategically, and boost their comprehension skills (Purcell-Gates, Duke, and Martineau 2007).

## How We Can Recruit Parents as Children's Partners, Not Taskmasters, in Summer Reading

Simply providing books that fit students' interests and ability *does* significantly improve most students' reading performance, but the addition of parent support along with teacher scaffolding may result in greater growth (White and Kim 2008). Although this was not studied against a control group, it was one part of an approach that was effective overall. In their study, the researchers structured parent support by asking parents to listen to their child read a short 100-word passage aloud and to ask their child about the book. Parents then completed a postcard that included their perceptions of their children's fluency, as well as questions for students to answer, such as "Did you finish reading this book?" and "What did you do to better understand this book?" (120). The postcards were then mailed to the researchers. Given the success of this approach in this study, this technique seems replicable for classroom teachers as a way to structure parent support of summer reading.

**For more ideas on how parents can support summer reading**

see Section 3, page 56

## How Personal Goals and Opportunities to Collaborate Can Keep Children Motivated

All the supports for summer reading that we've explained are based on that essential force: motivation. Motivation is not a switch that stays on but a fire that must be fed. Earlier in the chapter we cited Guthrie and Humenick's (2004) meta-analysis (see Figure 2–3) to demonstrate the importance of providing students with interesting books and allowing students to choose the books that are read. Two other elements were also significant motivators—*personal knowledge goals* and *collaboration*. Just as important in promoting engagement, and ultimately, reading achievement, was the opportunity to develop personal goals, or quests for knowledge about a particular topic, and the opportunity to collaborate. In proposing "seven rules of engagement," Gambrell (2012) also described *social interaction* with others about what has been read as a cornerstone of motivation and necessary part of recreational reading.

**For details on how to make this project work for your classroom**

see Section 3, pages 63

A recent pen pal project developed by Gambrell and her colleagues (2011) suggests how social interaction might be facilitated when school is not in session. In this project, which took place during the school year, 280 students in grades 3–5 received a narrative and informational book to keep and read. Students wrote and received letters from an adult in which they (students and adults) discussed books read in common. Students also talked about the books with their peers at school and they discussed the letters that they wrote and received. When asked what they liked best about the project the majority of the students (78 percent) said they liked having a pen pal and sending and getting letters and talking with their peers about the book. In response to a question about what they learned, students claimed they learned "new things," understood the book better, and liked sharing ideas. The researchers noted that the students' responses supported the theory that interaction, as in discussion and letter exchanges, enabled the learner to "appropriate the tools for understanding" (251). By talking with or writing to others who may be more skilled, students were able to move through their developmental comfort zone and understand books that initially may have been challenging for them.

Being able to talk about books or write about books and share that information with others, and being able to borrow, trade, or otherwise exchange books with others are some of the ways that social interaction can come into play, even during the summer months. As Gambrell and her colleagues noted, "authentic literacy tasks have the potential to support and sustain literacy motivation" (2011, 251), and we assert that authentic interactions around books can take place during summers. The essential framework of the pen pal project can transfer to other ways of collaborating—they just require a little planning. Figure 2–9 gives an overview of how to ensure summer-reading success.

> **For practices that support talking and writing about books**
>
> see Section 3

**Figure 2–9    An Overview of How to Plan for Summer-Reading Success**

| An Overview of How to Plan for Summer-Reading Success |
| --- |
| • Give kids a lot of book choices: <br>     ➢ diverse topics <br>     ➢ diverse genres <br>     ➢ a wide range of reading levels <br> • Make it happen every summer. <br> • Teach strategies to read and remember during the school year. <br> • Recruit parents as students' partners, not task masters, of summer reading. <br> • Boost engagement with social interaction—writing and/or talking about books. |

## Summer Reading Is Not Optional But Necessary

Let's admit that many of us—parents, teachers, school leaders—have at one moment in time thought that it would be nice if children read during the summer, but that it's out of our hands. At this time, few schools and even fewer districts have developed or implemented plans that foster the kinds of summer interventions that substantively affect literacy development. Although we grind our teeth when people thoughtlessly give yet more work to teachers without acknowledging how full their plates already are, in this case, it's really important. We're asking you to take on the responsibility for summer reading because it will make such a big difference for so many children. We've shared information that demonstrates the essential role summer reading plays in literacy development and educational achievement and life chances for all students. We also know that children from more advantaged homes and neighborhoods are more likely to have easy access to books and more likely to read voluntarily during the summer months than children from less advantaged homes and neighborhoods. We know that we can increase voluntary reading and reading achievement for children from economically disadvantaged homes and high-poverty neighborhoods by simply increasing their access to books. In fact, poor children who live in households where few books are present benefit the most from summer projects that provide access to books. In addition to issues of poverty, summer reading ensures that reading becomes a practice that all children own. They read for themselves—to find out who they are, to find out about the world, and to grow and develop as people. And that's our goal for every student. Our study and those of others present a compelling case for the benefits that accrue to students from first grade through elementary school who actually read during the summer and the characteristics of book projects that support children to do so. We've laid out the thirty-plus years of research that explains why summer reading is necessary—and what you can do to support it. In the next section, you'll find how to make this work for your own students, as well as ideas for schoolwide implementation.

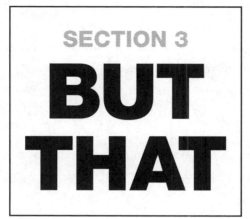

## SECTION 3

# BUT THAT

## School-Year Practices and Summer Projects That Support Summer Reading

### CARRIE CAHILL and KATHY HORVATH

Albert Einstein once said, "Intellectuals solve problems; geniuses prevent them." Great educators show genius. These teachers read professional journals, collaborate with colleagues, and use data, including daily observations of student work and behavior, to make informed decisions about what students need to improve. Teachers enable children to leap over obstacles by anticipating and addressing them. We see these signs of genius in classrooms every day.

In Section 2, you learned that summer-reading loss is an obstacle that teachers can prevent. Although we're suggesting that the individual teacher take on part of this responsibility, the metaphor for this work is best described as a relay race, a collaboration between one grade-level teacher and the next. In a relay race, the baton is passed from runner to runner within the same meet. As one runner is reaching his or her finish line, another begins to jog and reaches back for the handoff from his or her teammate. The flow is continuous without an obvious stop and restart. As one teacher is closing the year, we are proposing certain summer extensions to bridge the months and keep students reading. These students are passed on to the next teacher in a continuous flowing movement without the summer vacation interrupting the flow of reading. We use this metaphor as an invitation to imagine what effective summer-reading practice can look like. In this section, we'll offer a variety of practices that instill the habits of avid readers in all your students—strong habits that can compete with other influences of summer, which range from being a couch potato to playing baseball and taking trips to the zoo.

## Foster Habits of Independence During the School Year

**Want to know the research that supports strategy instruction?**

see Section 2, page 38

The prevention of summer-reading loss actually starts during the school year itself. Teachers can build students' stamina for independent reading during the summer by supporting independent reading during the school year. The Gradual Release of Responsibility (Pearson and Gallagher 1983)—"I do it, we do it, you do it"—informs these practices, allowing for an appropriate balance (based on student needs) of teacher modeling with time for students to apply the concepts taught both individually and with peers. Shared reading experiences create community around reading and engage students. The teacher shows that challenge is part of reading and demonstrates reading strategies that help the reader move from confusion to understanding and that deepen comprehension. Through strategy instruction, students learn that reading is a complex process that involves careful, deliberate steps in making meaning. Students are then given lots of opportunities to practice these strategies in small groups and individually with the teacher's guidance. When this process is repeated time and time again during the school year, students develop the behaviors of stronger and more independent readers, which they can put to work in the summer (see Figure 3–1).

**Figure 3–1**  School-Year Practices That Develop Summer Readers

| School-Year Practices That Develop Summer Readers |
|---|

Spend 90–120 minutes each day on growing independent readers by using these practices:

- Read/Think-Aloud/Crafting (minilesson: strategy and skill)

- Interactive Read/Think-Aloud (minilesson with turn and talk, pair shares)

- Shared Reading (choral read, response share, common text)

- Composing/Practicing/Building Independence (30–50 minutes)

  ➤ Teacher conducts small-group reading and invitational groups

  ➤ Teacher confers with individual students

  ➤ Students may read independently, with partners, or in small groups (book discussions and application of learning)

    — Book club/literature circles

    — Application of deep and surface structures

    — Composing written responses to text

    — Analyze a text for an author's purpose or craft

- Reunite Whole Group/Reflections

  ➤ Peer sharing and wrap-up

  ➤ Student reflection

Adapted from *To Understand* (Keene 2007)

| Teacher Practices | Student Behaviors |
|---|---|
| Expose students to a variety of texts through genre studies through teacher read-alouds and independent reading choices. | Develop and discuss preferences for certain genres and experience reading for pleasure. |
| Model reading behaviors outside of school by sharing personal "bedside table" reading such as novels, magazines, and technical/professional reading. | Expand repertoire and purposes for reading. |

*(continues)*

**Figure 3-1** (*continued*)

| Teacher Practices | Student Behaviors |
|---|---|
| Teach techniques used by various authors to engage the reader and use author's series to hook students. | Build a habit of reading a series of books by the same author and develop personal preferences for certain types of texts and understandings about craft. |
| Integrate science and social studies topics into literacy instruction; create excitement for reading informational texts for independent reading. Build curiosity for reading related titles. | Reach for informational text anytime they are curious about a topic, not just during a certain school subject. |
| Develop student interests in particular topics by encouraging further inquiry based on questions that the students ask. Perhaps there are themes or topics in which students would like to explore beyond the curriculum or in preparation for the next school year. | Develop a habit for researching topics of interest. Students can also build their knowledge and schema for the areas of study that they will learn in future classes. |
| Reread class favorites and support student choice to read these titles during independent reading. | Enjoy rereading favorite texts in school and at home. Students will tend to be successful with these texts, even if they are slightly more difficult than their usual texts. |
| Seek out and discuss titles throughout the year in which students have developed an interest. Perhaps the teacher can host a "Book Spotlight" session every few weeks. The teacher can also encourage students to highlight certain titles that they have found interesting as a whole-class or small-group activity. | Explore lots of titles and shape preferences for certain types of texts. Develop skills in evaluating texts and identifying components that make certain texts more interesting reads. |

| Teacher Practices | Student Behaviors |
|---|---|
| Host student (individual or small-group) book reviews that can be videotaped or made into webcasts and accessed by students throughout the school year-round. | Develop the practices of seeking out book recommendations from their peers or sharing their own reviews. |

Maybe all or most of this list in Figure 3–1 is familiar to you and your students during the school year, but do you explicitly talk about how these practices will be part of students' summer-reading practices? When we make that connection explicit, repeatedly, we not only explain what students' summer reading will look like but set an expectation that it will happen.

Social interaction gives purpose to these practices. By talking and writing about books with a real and important audience, their peers, students learn that reading can be part of their social identity. These conversations about books help students further develop their understanding of what they have read. When teachers ask students to reflect on their reading habits and identity as readers, they're getting students to understand how reading is part of who they are. We want children to see how reading is a way to define who they can be. It is an expansive, joyful experience that helps them grow their own thinking and connect to other people. If, during the school year, students can learn that reading is joyful, that it can be a tool to express and develop their identity and something they can get better at, then they'll keep doing it during the summer.

**Why is social interaction an important component of reading?**

see Section 2, pages 40–41

## What Successful Independent Readers Look Like, One Teacher's Experience

*"Last summer I made a quick stop at the local library to drop off some books when I spotted four of my former students huddled together in a small reading room in the back. I peeked in to say hello. The students were so glad to see me and couldn't wait to share that this was their weekly summer book club meeting. They told me that they loved reading and talking with each other about books in my class so much that they wanted to keep it going over the summer. They meet each Thursday morning for an hour at the library to discuss their latest finds. They invited me to join them. I sat for a few minutes, not as a teacher, but as a fellow reader. I was so proud that these students had extended the routine that we developed in class to their daily lives. I finally understood the term* lifelong reader.*"*

**Jim, a fifth-grade teacher**

## Celebrate the Variety of Texts and Topics Students Choose to Read

Spring can become a time to plant the seeds for summer reading. By reviewing favorite titles from the year, students are reminded of their preferences and the joy of reading and think about what they may want to reread during the summer. Teachers should emphasize the variety of text—not just different kinds of books, topics, and genres—but magazines, websites, and other media that were part of that year's school reading.

**How can personal knowledge goals motivate students to read?**

see Section 2, page 40

We can encourage students to identify personal knowledge goals—interesting topics or questions that have arisen from their experiences during the year. These inquiries can help students launch summer investigations. By further exploring and reading about topics they have chosen, students are motivated to search for texts, websites, or magazines to gain a deeper understanding of the topic and seek answers to their questions. Before the school year ends, teachers can help students find partners who share their passion for certain topics or who desire to know more about an idea. Students can get together with their partners over the summer to do research or just connect with each other about what they have discovered.

In addition, teachers should feel free to reintroduce books previously read during the school year and make them available for summer reading. Rereading is an authentic and worthy habit, and many students, especially those who struggle, are likely to choose familiar titles to read independently. When students have developed their schema for books that have been read aloud several times, they generally find more success when reading them independently, even if the books are slightly more difficult than the student is typically able to read. Students who are encouraged to read those books multiple times during the summer are also increasing their reading fluency and comprehension.

## Put Books in Children's Hands

Ensuring that books are readily available to students when they are at home can seem like a daunting task. Often, struggling readers and students from low-socioeconomic families have fewer books in their homes. Furthermore, they may not have the resources—money to buy books or well-stocked public libraries—to gain access to popular titles or books of interest. While access to books is an obstacle in stemming summer-reading loss, it is not a hopeless situation. Over the years, we have witnessed many creative educators get books into children's hands. The following ideas are a collection of innovations from these educators.

> **Want to know why putting books in kids' hands is essential for summer reading success?**
>
> see Section 2, page 19

## Look for Funds Within Your School Community

Contact your school PTO or PTA to seek support in purchasing titles for summer-reading books. PTOs, along with other school groups, often sponsor book fairs during the school year, which can be a source of revenue and/or donations for summer books. Usually there is an option to buy one book and get one free, rather than to earn a profit from selling books. Perhaps students could purchase one book for themselves and choose another free book for the summer-reading collection. Book fair companies also give many free books as a bonus for scheduling a fair and include even more free books when a certain quota has been achieved. This could be a schoolwide project in which all students can make a difference.

## Reach Out to Local Businesses

Work with one of the organizations or businesses in the community to host a book drive. Most likely, the local Chamber of Commerce would be happy to assist. Many businesses are searching for opportunities to get more involved in the community. Some even have a policy that their employees must do community service a specific number of times per year. The business could post the number of books that they donated to local schools on their windows, websites, and advertisements. Students could also write thank-you letters to the companies that can also be displayed throughout their company. Many schools have electronic signs and/or newsletters where they can publically thank the business for their donations. These types of activities build community spirit.

In Carrie's district, a group of teachers coordinated a gently used book drive in partnership with the community food pantry. Book drop-off sites were set up in supermarkets and other local stores. In the month of May alone, the teachers collected 2,540 books. These books were proudly delivered to the local food pantry. This activity provided needy families with nourishment for the body *and* mind.

## Get Help from Professional Organizations

Many professional organizations such as the local School Business Officials Association or your state School Boards Association fund various reading projects. Several teachers from a local school district have been awarded funds to purchase books for students to take home over the summer. Local and regional reading councils offer mini-grants for teachers with creative ideas for summer reading and family reading opportunities.

One first-grade reading specialist in Midlothian, Illinois, Ellen, wrote and received a grant from one of the organizations listed above. Her project, entitled "You've Got Mail," involved mailing home books over the summer that were related to topics her students expressed interest in during the year. She mailed three books in July and three in August to each of her students. She included a handwritten note to each encouraging them to read and enjoy their book and a small journal for them to record their thoughts about the books. In the fall, most of her students returned the journals for Ellen to read. The books were theirs to keep. Parents expressed gratitude and commented that their children hadn't enjoyed reading that much in the past. This year, Ellen is going to reapply for the same grant, but add a few components. She wants to hold a launch party with parents to ensure that they understand the project and build excitement when the package of books arrives in the mail. A family celebration will also be planned in the fall where students will share the books they read and some of their favorite highlights.

## Partner with Your Local Library

Community libraries are great resources for children. Because many districts in low-socioeconomic neighborhoods do not have building librarians, schools may choose to partner with their local libraries. They may be willing to set up a lending system for students during the summer. Besides housing thousands of titles, they have knowledgeable staff that can talk about the books and help students choose according to their interests.

You can also ask your community library about programs that are in place to reach low-socioeconomic students in the area, as some schools serve students from more than one community. One or more of those communities may not have their own library. It would be helpful if the local library would consider reaching beyond the boundaries of their particular municipality so that all students in the school could be allowed to check out books.

## Collect Books from Book Depositories

Many communities also have book depositories. This is a warehouse where schools, businesses, and individuals drop off books at their convenience. These books are stored year-round. Teachers can obtain books at no cost from these depositories. One such place is called *Scarce* in Glen Ellyn, Illinois, a self-described "book rescue zone." Their goal is to rescue books from the landfills and get them into the hands of children. They depend on donations to keep their doors open. Teachers can take as many books as they can fit into their car so that they can be shared with their students.

## Invite Guest Readers to Share and Donate Favorite Books

Guest readers have graced many of our classrooms over the years. A creative twist can be asking the visitors to bring a book of their choice that they will leave for the summer book collection. Some teachers work with the local high schools to have graduates come back to read to the children in their classrooms. Many high schools require their students to earn hours toward community service. This is an excellent way to meet this requirement while serving the younger children in the neighborhood. To make it even more impactful, returning students are asked to wear their uniforms or clothing that represents a particular high school sport, club, or activity when they come to read. The picture that is presented to our young students is powerful. Seeing high school students reading to younger children while wearing their band uniform, football jersey, or costume from a play demonstrates that teens with all different interests have the love of reading in common.

Senior citizens are some of the best guest readers for schools. They often have time during the school day to come into classrooms. They also can serve as the grandparents that many children have never experienced. Schools can make arrangements for senior citizens to come to the buildings twice a week in the summer and read with students. The connections made can be long lasting and be beneficial for both parties. And these relationships can be maintained over the summer if senior citizens volunteer for reading time at the local library, community center, or school.

## Get More Books with Twenty-First-Century Tools

Thanks to the wonders of technology, there are many new possibilities for bringing texts to students electronically. These opportunities open doors for students by allowing access to rich literature at their fingertips.

**Explore websites for classroom donations.** Sites like Donors Choose (www.donorschoose.org) invite teachers to write brief proposals describing a need for their classrooms or an educational project. Other sites include Teacher Wish Lists (www.teacherwishlists.com) and Adopt a Classroom (www.adoptaclassroom.org). Donors then search the many proposals and decide which ideas they want to fund. Many of the teachers in our school districts have made requests that have been granted. Literacy-related donations seem to be very popular. Teachers have received numerous tablets and e-readers, which have gone a long way in encouraging reluctant readers. One teacher in particular received funds to create "take-home literacy bags" for her students. Who knows, maybe someone famous like Oprah Winfrey or Bill Gates will fund your next classroom project!

**E-readers.** More and more schools are using grant funds to purchase Kindles or Nooks and make them available to students. Schools download various titles, and students can check out the e-readers for independent reading at school and at home. These devices can be lent to students for the summer to provide them with access to texts. Most library systems allow their books to be checked out electronically on Kindles and Nooks. This technology gives students access to a wealth of titles without having to leave home. Of course, these devices are expensive and can access inappropriate content, so teachers need to communicate clearly with students and teachers about the care and supervised use of these devices. An Internet search for "child safety" on these devices will provide step-by-step guidelines on setting up adult/parental control of appropriate content.

**For a list of some of the most popular books for kids**

see Section 2, pages 30, 32–33

**Library audiobooks.** Libraries also have audiobooks available. This can be a very effective tool for students who struggle or may be reluctant to read lengthier texts. Students are motivated to read popular books that their peers are reading. Often, these books are too difficult for struggling readers to tackle independently. Audiobooks are vehicles for making it possible for all students to have read the latest pop culture book, fantasy novel, or intriguing mystery series. Audiobooks open the door for these students to join in the conversation with others. Struggling readers can be part of the social circle talking about the latest novel. They no longer need to wait for the movie to be part of the discussion. Furthermore, when the movie does come out, they can be a part of the dialogue comparing the book to the movie. It is a win-win!

One of the largest providers of audiobooks, Learning Ally, was started by a woman in the 1940s who wanted to supply audiobooks to soldiers who lost their sight in combat. The not-for-profit organization became known as Reading for the Blind. The organization changed its name to Learning Ally in 2011. When Carrie's school district was awarded a grant to provide reading opportunities for students with disabilities, they purchased iPods for all special education classrooms. They filled the iPods with downloaded audiobooks from Learning Ally in June, right before the students left for summer break. Students packed up their desks and went home with their loaded iPods. Each child received a print copy of the downloaded book so that they could follow the words on the page while they listened.

The following September, parents of these students came to Open House with tears in their eyes describing the sense of accomplishment their child had after reading their first books. They went on to say that their children read more books that summer than they ever had in their lifetime. These children have continued their voracious appetite for books throughout the school year. The program was so successful that enhancements are planned. For example, because the students had iPods, they might text each other thoughts they're having while they're reading.

Figure 3–2 offers a starter list of ideas to ensure that students have access to books throughout the summer.

**Figure 3–2   Resources for Increasing Student Access to Books**

| Resources | Options |
|-----------|---------|
| PTO or PTA organizations | Host a book fair: buy one, get one free. Coordinate a book drive. Attend a meeting and bring a book. Sponsor "Donate a Book on Each Student's Birthday" schoolwide program (these books can be collected for summer reading). |
| Book depositories | Locate a book depository in your area where educators are able to take free books. Establish a school team that makes a visit each quarter. |

*(continues)*

**Figure 3–2** (*continued*)

| Resources | Options |
|---|---|
| Websites for grants | Check out popular websites including Donors Choose, Adopt a Classroom, and Teacher Wish Lists. |
| | Investigate local and national sections of the International Reading Association. |
| Libraries | Create a partnership to ensure that print books and audiobooks are accessible for all students. |
| | Coordinate a schedule for librarians to showcase specific titles or genres throughout the summer. |
| | Create a checkout system so that themed book bags can be created and selected by students from the school. |
| School-to-school partnerships | School districts with a greater amount of resources annually inventory the books in their building libraries and clear some shelves for the newer releases. These schools welcome the opportunity to distribute their extra copies to other districts. |
| Partnerships with local businesses | Businesses may donate funds for books. |
| | Bookstores may donate books or gift cards for summer purchases. |
| Classroom libraries | Develop a summer checkout system for books from classroom libraries. Usually, these books are boxed up at the end of a year until the fall. Also, books used in summer school can be added to a checkout collection. |

## Make Reading a Family Affair

Many parents have expressed frustration with their children's perceptions of reading as only a school-based activity, but it doesn't have to be that way. Here are some ideas to engage parents in positive ways.

## Book Bags and Collaborative Journals

Sending home book bags with students can provide access to books throughout the summer. Book bags can be theme-based so that the texts relate to a specific genre, such as mysteries, or topic, such as reptiles or natural disasters. Children can choose from among the books in the theme.

To help guide choice, teachers and librarians can do book chats about the books within the bags before the school year ends, during summer school, or during any summer-reading event. Include a journal for recording the family's impressions of the books in each book bag. Each time a new family checks out the bag, they can read the comments of the previous families and add their own. In addition, parents may also be asked to fill out a survey about what they learned from reading the books with their child and to rate the experience. This enables teachers to follow up on how families are responding to the literacy bag and to see if any changes need to be made to help everyone get the most out of the experience. School personnel can monitor which books are actually being read by the students, and when one book bag is returned, another one can be checked out.

> **Why are social interactions like this collaborative journal valuable supports for summer reading?**
>
> see Section 2, page 40

## "Breakfast and Books"

Schools can schedule "Breakfast and Books" events once a month over the summer, inviting students and parents to sit and read together or discuss favorite books while nibbling on bagels and sipping juice boxes. Book baskets are on the tables so that all families have access to books. Local businesses can be a sponsor of such events, providing food and/books.

## Scaffold Social Interaction for Students

When adult readers encounter a book they love, they have to talk about it. There are many ways to honor this authentic reading habit, but here are a few gems we've seen teachers use with great success.

## Book Sharing

On the last day of school this year, Kathy walked into several first-grade classrooms expecting to see students helping to pack up the classroom for the summer. Instead, much to her delight, she found first graders sitting or lying down sharing their favorite books with a partner from another class. The teachers explained that they were pairing students from different first grades so that they could get to know other students who may be their classmates in the second grade. It was a spectacular and replicable example of teachers culminating one school year and preparing for a smooth transition into the next by introducing new friends and socializing around favorite books. What could be more fun than talking about a favorite book with a new friend? There are many ways we can keep that fun going through blogs (see below) or weekly/monthly partner or group gatherings. Give students a calendar to map out these peer interactions and think about making guest appearances to help ensure commitment and so that you can enjoy witnessing their independence and growth.

## Student Blogs

Teachers can encourage discussion and book-centric socializing by developing a blog during the school year and maintaining it throughout the summer. The teacher moderates the blog by asking questions to help propel discussion, but they favor the role of participant, chatting about the books that they are reading. Teachers can share the moderation responsibilities with teachers in the coming grade level to create a cross-grade-level community, which will help students more smoothly transition to the reading in that teacher's classroom in the fall. This forum enables students and teachers to share impressions of books and make recommendations to each other. Parents are welcome to join the discussions, as well.

To design student blogs, go to http://kidblog.org/home/. This site provides a simple approach for teachers from kindergarten through high school to create student blogs. Students can publish, post, and participate in book discussions in a secure location. Teachers can have complete control over student blogs and user accounts, keeping the conversations academic and focused on learning. The most exciting news for teachers is that there is no cost. This type of activity allows teachers to provide scaffolded learning from the comfort of their own homes.

## ePals

Teachers can create online partnerships through ePals (http://ePals.com), a great option for students who prefer to talk one on one with a peer rather than a whole group. Students can find an ePal from two hundred different countries around the world. Some students are more comfortable getting feedback from a friend first, before blogging to the whole group, so having the opportunity to have a single ePal for sharing can be a great step before blogging with a large group.

## Preexisting Blogs and Websites

Teachers and students can also enjoy social interaction through existing blogs and websites, reading and posting reviews, as well as finding resources on books. There is a blog out there for everyone. GuysLitWire (http://guyslitwire.blogspot.com/), for example, reviews books mainly for boys. There are book recommendations, downloadable audiobooks, comic books, and comic book reviews, to name a few. Another blog is sponsored by National Geographic: http://kidsblogs.nationalgeographic.com/blog/dogeared/. This site requires parental permission for students to make comments. Children write reviews and make book recommendations. The site www.spaghettibookclub.org is not only a place where students write and share book reviews, but they can even draw a picture about the book and include it with their review.

Heather, a fifth-/sixth-grade teacher in Midlothian, Illinois, exposes her students to the wide variety of book and author blogs through the use of her SMART Board beginning in August of each school year. She forms book clubs based on student interests: topics, authors, and so on.

These clubs give her students an audience and purpose for their reading, which especially benefits her reluctant readers. The continuity of blogs helps emphasize that reading is an ongoing activity, as students can continue to maintain the blog through the next school year.

There are so many Internet websites that can empower students to have a voice and share their thinking and recommendations about the books that they are reading. Teachers and students can go to www.scholastic.com and find many links to blogs and message boards for budding writers to try out their craft. This same website has a link called Share What You're Reading, which can be accessed by going to http://teacher.scholastic.com/activities/swyar/. This site gives students a place to post reviews on books they've read and to read posts by other children their own age from all over the nation. Posted reviews are sorted by grade level so children can go to age appropriate reviews, if they desire. This site also offers students advice and tips from real authors on the elements of a good book review. Teachers can consult this website to see what students across the country are doing and bring that to life in their classrooms during the school year or during a summer school program.

## Postcards

**For more on the research that supports this practice**

see Section 2, page 40

For those who are less technologically inclined or for students who may not have access to computers over the summer, the classroom teacher can distribute postcards with the school address on the label. Students can be asked to mail back the postcards sharing their reactions to books, if they would recommend them to other students, and what type of audience would most appreciate the book. Some teachers pass out a list of award-winning titles and ask students to consider reading some of them to provide feedback.

Some schools have a phone alert system that enables school officials to send out mass notifications to all students or to particular groups of students. Fellow educators have shared with us that their principal sends out messages during the summer ranging from general statements encouraging students to continue reading to specific shout-outs to students who have returned a book review postcard so the whole grade can benefit from their recommendations.

Students are excited to hear that their recommendations will help determine which books the teacher highlights to his or her new class in the fall. Some of the responses can be posted in the classroom so that students new to that grade can read the comments. Peer-to-peer referrals are powerful motivators.

## Recommendation Notebooks

At one elementary school, summer reading at every grade level includes students writing a brief notebook entry for each book stating the title, author, genre, brief highlights of the book, and an explanation of whether they'd recommend the book to their peers. At the beginning of the school year, student responses were posted throughout the school, including classrooms, hallways, the library, lunchroom, and so on. This collection of recommendations by students for students became a resource for students as they continued their independent reading lives in the fall. Because students knew the importance of these recommendations as a resource for their peers, the recommendations were thoughtful and specific, and the abundance of the recommendations themselves helped to emphasize the value and reality of choice. But the recommendations weren't just a resource for students; teachers reviewed the recommendations for ideas of potential read-alouds during the school year and new books to acquire for school and classroom libraries, as well as specific information about who their new students were as readers. This type of summer practice also provides the new grade-level teacher with a great deal of information regarding each

> **Why are shared book experiences among peers a powerful motivator to read?**
>
> see Section 2, page 41

student's preferences for reading. When helping reluctant readers choose what to read, these recommendations became a valuable peer resource, one where they could use peer relationships as a lever into reading: "I know you and Victor like many of the same things, let's see what he recommends."

## Write to Authors

Teachers can also encourage students to think about and discuss their author preferences. During the school year, teachers can help students establish correspondence with a favorite author. This communication can continue throughout the summer and into the new school year. As the student is exposed to new titles, the teacher at that grade level can assist the student in contacting new authors.

A fifth-grade student in Midlothian, Illinois, brought this idea to life. It all started with a class pumpkin-decorating contest in the fall. Students were asked to carve a pumpkin in the likeness of their favorite book character. Some of the finished products included Harry Potter, various princesses, and loads of sports figures. One student, Dante, carved a pumpkin with a beard and hat. When Dante presented his pumpkin to the class, he proudly declared, "My favorite character from a book is Ralph Fletcher as himself—from his memoir *Marshfield Dreams*" (2005). Ralph Fletcher's book had been used as the mentor text during the class memoir study. Dante's choice reminded his teacher how much read-alouds can launch students' independent reading lives. Recognizing a powerful opportunity to strengthen his identity as a reader, she looked on the Internet for Ralph Fletcher's email address and sent the author a message that included a picture of Dante's pumpkin and some questions from him about the writing process. Within days, Ralph Fletcher responded. He answered Dante's questions and said that he was going to look into purchasing a distinguished hat for himself like the one Dante had portrayed him wearing. This one email led to further correspondence between Mr. Fletcher and Dante that extended throughout the summer and the next school year. Their relationship changed Dante as a reader (and writer). Dante read every book by Ralph Fletcher that he could get his hands on and even went on to write his own stories inspired by Fletcher's writing.

At a summer school event where students were allowed to choose a book as a reward, Dante immediately picked *Marshfield Dreams*. When asked why he chose this book, because everyone knew he had already read it, he responded, "Yes, but I don't own my own copy!" When Ralph Fletcher completed his latest book, *Guy-Write, What Every Guy Writer Needs to Know* (2012), Dante was one of the first to receive an autographed copy. This relationship of two guy readers and writers continues to flourish!

## Support Personal Learning Goals

Mindi, a teacher in a Northbrook School District outside of Chicago, asks her students to create a summer-reading plan during the last two weeks of school. Students include their genre and author preferences, reading goals for the summer, book clubs in which they will participate, and procedures for sharing book recommendations

**How do personal learning goals support summer reading?**

see Section 2, page 40

with their teacher and other students throughout the summer. Mindi confers with each student to ensure they have a realistic, achievable plan. By developing personal goals, choosing their own texts, and knowing that they will be communicating their thinking with each other during the summer, Mindi's students are motivated to keep reading when school is not in session. A class blog becomes a home base for this work as Mindi checks in with students for updates. This simple support and community space nudges students to keep reading.

In the fall, the students present their plans and evidence of their achievements to the new teacher. In a sense, the student is telling the new teacher who he is and what is important to him as a reader. This plan can be a great springboard for developing reading goals for the start of the new school year and creates a seamless transition that communicates the value of year-round reading. It also demonstrates a team approach for instruction.

## The School Is the Hub for Learning Year-Round

These ideas tell the story of the influence of individual teachers and schools on stemming summer-reading loss. When teachers collaborate together, they can remind students that school is more than a building they attend September through June, but a group of people who support students' growth and independence even when students are not there. With a little effort, school can even literally become a place for student learning during the summer.

While teachers are hosting blogs, the school can identify certain dates for student book clubs to meet. These groups can be facilitated by teachers, the principal, parent volunteers, or other school support personnel. Student groups can be developed before summer begins based on student interests, the contents of the reading plans, favorite genres, or popular authors. For younger children, parent and child book clubs can be held. Otherwise, adult book talks can be held simultaneously, while their children meet in another room.

We're offering a different vision of the school during the summer than traditional summer school, which educators and parents often believe is the grand solution to poor academic achievement. There has been considerable research and many approaches to summer school. It is beyond the scope of this book to discuss the research and practice in this area, but suffice it to say that summer school should be viewed as potentially complementing, but not replacing, a schoolwide focus on summer reading among all students. Unfortunately, not all summer programs are well designed or value a concentrated focus on reading. Even the most effective summer programs sometimes communicate the idea of reading as a school-related activity. If there's one thing we cannot emphasize enough, it is the importance of developing the habit of independent reading.

## Embrace Your Own Ingenuity

The ideas we've shared are invitations to invent. We're always looking to others for new and creative ways to foster the joy of reading, and we know you've got more to add to our list. Following the principles that research has given us, we can use our experience and creativity to break the cycle of summer-reading loss. By incorporating a few thoughtful activities, educators can bridge the gap and develop year-round readers, rather than school-dependent readers. Aligned with Albert Einstein's words, let's solve summer-reading loss by preventing it with a few ingenious, but practical ideas.

# AFTERWORD

ELLIN OLIVER KEENE

How do we imagine our own summer-reading lives? As Nell suggested in the introduction, most of us look forward to reading at our own pace, perhaps gobbling some books and lingering over others. More than a relationship with ink and paper or our Kindle, we look forward to time with authors. We hear characters' voices in our heads and empathize with their dilemmas; we explore a question that has been needling us or explore new places and ideas. And, when we put down a book, we come away with some new understanding that matters to us and our communities. In that time with books in our hands, fingers on keyboards probing a topic further, hours evaporate and by the time we look up, we might be sitting in the same place, but our minds have experienced movement, growth. We relish the thought of this immersion in the life of the mind and count the days until we're free to experience it.

As you're now aware, children may not share our positive feelings about summer reading or they may not have access to the books and tools that will make it possible for them to lose themselves in several months of reading and learning. The authors of this book have shown with clarity that the loss many children experience in the summer is significant and preventable. And they have lavished readers with doable ideas that can turn our dreams of summer reading into reality for children across the country.

I hope that the research and practices in this book will give you the confidence to begin talking with your students about the joy and value of summer reading. These conversations can begin in September and build up like a great plot line toward the excitement of summer reading. I know that we don't have to accept a falling plot line toward stagnant summer months. The resolution can be significant increases in the time and quality of children's engagement with text over the summer. But we need to begin now.

I can imagine children gathered around teachers and librarians, principals and parents talking about how it will feel to read outside, where they can find books to fall in love with, how they can connect with other readers to explore ideas, how their choices about what to read are as wide as that summer sky, and what gifts they'll bring as they march into the next grade with bigger bodies and stronger minds.

I know that these adult guides will need to be explicit about how to *continue* to be a thoughtful, strategic reader with a wide range of tactics to use should text become challenging. I know we'll remind children until the minute they clamor out the door in June about their strengths and skillfulness as readers; we'll be specific about what they *can* do as readers and how they can make reading a part of their lives. We will work to ensure that our words of clarity and encouragement accompany them into the summer warmth.

On behalf of the four authors of this title and our wonderful series editor, Margaret LaRaia, Nell and I believe that this book will make a difference and that we can all—teachers and children—imagine a summer life with books, wherever that may be.

# REFERENCES

## Children's Works Cited

Arnold, T. 2005. *Fly Guy*. New York: Cartwheel Books.

Behling, S. 2004. *How to Draw Spiderman*. New York: Scholastic.

Bridges, R. 2003. *Ruby Bridges*. New York: Scholastic.

Capucilli, A. S. 1999. *Biscuit*. New York: HarperCollins.

Clarke, P., T. Riley, and M. Bergin. 2003. *Scary Creatures: Big Cats*. Danbury, CT: Scholastic.

Collins, S. 2010. *Hunger Games*. New York: Scholastic.

Dower, L. 2003. *Hangin' with Hilary Duff*. New York: Scholastic.

Fletcher, Ralph. 2005. *Marshfield Dreams*. New York: Henry Holt.

———. 2012. *Guy-Write: What Every Guy Writer Needs to Know*. New York: Henry Holt.

Freidman, M. J. 2000. *Superman's First Flight*. New York: Scholastic.

Glass, E. 2001. *Pop People: Destiny's Child*. New York: Scholastic.

Holm, J. L. 2005. *Babymouse*. New York: Random House.

Hopkins, E. 2004. *Crank*. New York: Simon Pulse.

Jones, M. T., and D. Dudley. 2003. *Ghostville Elementary: New Ghoul in School*. New York: Scholastic.

Kinney, J. 2006. *Diary of a Wimpy Kid*. London: Penguin Books.

Lanier, B., and H. Goodyear. 2003. *Hey Lil' D: Take the Court*. New York: Scholastic.

Lanier, B., H. Goodyear, and D. Grover. 2003. *Hey Lil' D: It's All in the Name*. New York: Scholastic.

London, J., and F. Remkiewicz. 2000. *Froggy Goes to Bed*. New York: Puffin Books.

Martel, Yann. 2001. *Life of Pi*. Boston: Mariner Books/Houghton Mifflin Harcourt.

Medearis, A. S., D. Tate, and M. Galbreath. 2002. *What Did I Do to Deserve a Sister Like You?* Waco, TX: Eakin.

Meyer, S. 2005. *Twilight*. New York: Time–Warner.

Morreale, M. 2003. *Pop People: Lil' Romeo*. New York: Scholastic.

Numeroff, L. 1985. *If You Give a . . . .* New York: HarperCollins.

Osborne, M. P. 1992. *Magic Tree House*. Toronto: Random House.

Parish, P. 1992. *Amelia Bedelia*. New York: HarperCollins.

Park, B., and D. Brunkus. 2003. *Junie B. First Grader: Boss of Lunch*. New York: Random House.

Patterson, J. 2007. *Maximum Ride*. New York: Little, Brown.

Pilkey, D. 1999. *Captain Underpants and the Invasion of the Incredibly Naughty Cafeteria Ladies from Outer Space*. New York: Scholastic.

———. 2001. *The Captain Underpants Extra Crunchy Book o' Fun*. New York: Scholastic.

———. 2002. *The All New Captain Underpants Extra Crunchy Book o' Fun #2*. New York: Scholastic.

———. 2003. *Captain Underpants and the Big, Bad Battle of the Bionic Booger Boy*. New York: Scholastic.

———. 2003. *Captain Underpants and the Big, Bad Battle of the Bionic Booger Boy, part 2*. New York: Scholastic.

Pilkey, D., G. Beard, and H. Hutchins. 2002. *The Adventures of Super Diaper Baby*. New York: Scholastic.

Polacco, P. 1994. *Pink and Say*. New York: Philomel Books.

Preller, J. 2000. *Meet the Stars of Professional Wrestling*. New York: Scholastic.

Riordan, R. 2010. *Percy Jackson and the Olympians*. New York: Hyperion.

Rowling, J. K. 2000. *Harry Potter and the Goblet of Fire*. New York: Scholastic.

Royston, A. 2000. *Life Cycle of a Frog*. London: Dorling Kindersley.

Russell, R. R. 2009. *Dork Diaries*. New York: Aladdin.

Rylant, C. 1987. *Henry and Mudge*. New York: Simon & Schuster.

Sierra, J. 2000. *There's a Zoo in Room 22*. Orlando, FL: Harcourt.

Simon, S. 2001. *Animals Nobody Loves*. San Francisco: Chronicle Books.

Smith, J. 2005. *Bone*. New York: Scholastic.

Smith, S. 2005. *Britney: The Unauthorized Biography of Britney Spears*. London: Pan MacMillan.

Snicket, Lemony. 2001. *Series of Unfortunate Events*. New York: HarperCollins.

Stine, R. L. 2004. *Goosebumps: Haunted Mask II*. New York: Scholastic.

Thaler, M., and J. Lee. 2004. *Black Lagoon*. New York: Scholastic.

von Ziegesar, C. 2002. *Gossip Girl*. New York: Warner.

Walsh, K. 2002. *Hangin' with Lil' Romeo*. New York: Scholastic.

Wood, D., and D. Cushman. 2000. *What Moms Can't Do*. New York: Simon & Schuster.

## Professional Works Cited

Alexander, K. L., D. R. Entwisle, and L. S. Olson. 2007. "Lasting Consequences of the Summer Learning Gap." *American Sociological Review* 72 (4): 167–80.

Allington, R. L., A. M. McGill-Franzen, G. Camilli, L. Williams, J. Graff, J. Zeig, C. Zmach, and R. Nowak. 2010. "Addressing Summer Reading Setback Among Economically Disadvantaged Elementary Students." *Reading Psychology* 31 (5): 411–27.

Bloom, H. S., C. Hill, A. R. Black, and M. W. Lipsey. 2008. *Performance Trajectories and Performance Gaps as Achievement Effect-Size Benchmarks for Educational Interventions*. MDRC Working Paper on Research Methodology. New York: MDRC.

Borman, G. D., G. M. Hewes, L. T. Overman, and S. Brown. 2003. "Comprehensive School Reform and Achievement: A Meta-Analysis." *Review of Educational Research* 73 (1): 125–39.

Bradley, R. H., R. F. Corwyn, H. P. McAdoo, and C. G. Coll. 2001. "The Home Environments of Children in the United States Part I: Variations by Age, Ethnicity, and Poverty Status." *Child Development* 72: 1844–67.

Chapman, M., M. Filipenko, M. McTavish, and J. Shapiro. 2007. "First Graders' Preferences for Narrative and/or Information Books and Perceptions of Other Boys' and Girls' Book Preferences." *Canadian Journal of Education* 30 (2): 531–45.

Coalition for Evidence-Based Policy. 2011. *Evidence Summary for Annual Book Fairs in High-Poverty Elementary Schools.* Available at http://evidencebasedprograms.org/1366-2/ annual-books-fairs-in-high-poverty-elementary-schools-near-top-tier.

Cooper, H., B. Nye, K. Charlton, J. Lindsay, and S. Greathouse. 1996. "The Effects of Summer Vacation on Achievement Test Scores: A Narrative and Meta-Analytic Review." *Review of Educational Research* 66 (3): 227–68.

Cooper, H., K. Charleton, J. C. Valentine, and L. Muhlenbruck. 2000. *Making the Most of Summer School: A Meta-Analytic and Narrative Review*, Vol. 65. Ann Arbor, MI: Society for Research in Child Development.

Constantino, R. 2005. "Print Environments Between High and Low Socioeconomic Status Communities." *Teacher Librarian* 32 (3): 22–25.

Dickinson, D., and J. DeTemple. 1998. "Putting Parents in the Picture: Maternal Reports of Preschoolers' Literacy as a Predictor of Early Reading." *Early Childhood Research Quarterly* 13: 241–61.

Dyson, A. H. 2003. *The Brothers and Sisters Learn to Write: Popular Literacies in Childhood and School Cultures*. New York: Teachers College Press.

Duke, N. K., P. D. Pearson, S. L. Strachan, and A. K. Billman. 2011. "Essential Elements of Fostering and Teaching Reading Comprehension." In *What Research Has to Say About Reading Instruction* (4th ed.), edited by S. J. Samuels and A. E. Farstrup, 51–93. Newark, DE: International Reading Association.

Duncan, G., and R. Murname, eds. 2011. *Wither Opportunity? Rising Inequality, Schools, and Children's Life Chances*. New York: The Russell Sage Foundation.

Edmiston, S. C. 2004. "A Look at Book-Mobile Services: Specific Groups and Outstanding Programs." *Book-Mobile and Outreach Services* 7 (1): 37–54.

Entwisle, D., K. Alexander, and L. Olson. 1997. *Children, Schools, and Inequality*. Boulder, CO: Westview Press.

Evans, M. D. R., J. Kelley, J. Sikora, and D. J. Treiman. 2010. "Family Scholarly Culture and Educational Success: Books and Schooling in 27 Nations." *Research in Social Stratification and Mobility* 28 (2): 171–97.

Fryer, R. G., and S. D. Levitt. 2002. *Understanding the Black-White Test Score Gap in the First Two Years of School*. Cambridge, MA: National Bureau of Economic Research.

Gambrell, L. 2012. "Seven Rules of Engagement." *The Reading Teacher* 65 (3): 172–78.

Gambrell, L., E. M. Hughes, L. Calvert, J. Malloy, and B. Igo. 2011. "Authentic Reading, Writing, and Discussion: An Exploratory Study of a Pen Pal Project." *The Elementary School Journal* 112 (2): 234–58.

Guthrie, J., and N. Humenick. 2004. "Motivating Students to Read: Evidence for Classroom Practices That Increase Reading Motivation and Achievement." In *The Voice of Evidence in Reading Research*, edited by P. McCardle and V. Chhabra, 329–54. Baltimore: Brookes.

Gutman, D. 2012. Foreword. In *What Kids Are Reading: The Book Reading Habits of Students in American Schools*, v–vi. Wisconsin Rapids, WI: Renaissance Learning.

Halle, T., B. Kurtz-Costes, and J. Mahoney. 1997. "Family Influences on School Achievement in Low-Socioeconomic, African-American Children." *Journal of Educational Psychology* 89: 527–37.

Hargis, C. 2006. "Setting Standards: An Exercise in Futility?" *Phi Delta Kappan* 87 (5): 393–95.

Heyns, B. 1978. *Summer Learning and the Effects of Schooling*. New York: Academic Press.

Keene, E. 2007. *To Understand*. Portsmouth, NH: Heinemann.

Kim, J. 2004. "Summer Reading and the Ethnic Achievement Gap." *Journal of Education of Students at Risk* 9 (2): 169–89.

Kim, J. 2006. "Effects of a Voluntary Summer Reading Intervention on Reading Achievement: Results from a Randomized Field Trial." *Educational Evaluation and Policy Analysis* 28 (4): 335–55.

Kinney, J. 2012. Introduction. In *What Kids Are Reading: The Book Reading Habits of Students in American Schools*, 1–2. Wisconsin Rapids, WI: Renaissance Learning.

Lindsay, J. 2013. "Interventions That Increase Children's Access to Print Material and Improve Their Reading Proficiencies." In *Summer Reading: Closing the Rich/Poor Achievement Gap*, edited by R. Allington and A. McGill-Franzen, 20–38. New York: Teachers College Press.

Malhoit, G. 2005. *Providing Rural Student's with a High Quality Education*. Arlington, VA: The Rural School and Community Trust.

Markwardt, Frederick C. Jr. 1998. *Peabody Individual Achievement Test—Revised: Normative Update*. Circle Pines, MN: American Guidance Service.

McGill-Franzen, A. 2009. "Series Books for Young Readers: Seeking Reading Pleasure and Developing Reading Competence." In *Children's Literature in the Reading Program: An Invitation to Read*, edited by D. Wooten and B. Cullinan, 57–65. Newark, DE: International Reading Association.

Mohr, K. 2003. "Children's Choices: A Comparison of Book Preferences Between Hispanic and Non-Hispanic First Graders." *Reading Psychology* 24 (2): 163–76.

———. 2006. "Children's Choices for Recreational Reading: A Three-Part Investigation of Selection Preferences, Rationales, and Processes." *Journal of Literacy Research* 38 (1): 81–104.

Neuman, S., and D. Celano. 2001. "Access to Print in Low-Income and Middle-Income Communities." *Reading Research Quarterly* 36: 8–26.

Pearson, P. David, and Margaret C. Gallagher. 1983. "The Instruction of Reading Comprehension." *Contemporary Educational Psychology* 8 (3): 317–44.

Pierce, J. B. 2007. "Buying into Gossip: Why Teens Consume Chick Lit." *American Libraries* 38 (4): 76.

Pilkey, D. 2012. "What Should Kids Be Reading?" In *What Kids Are Reading: The Book Reading Habits of Students in American Schools*, 28. Wisconsin Rapids, WI: Renaissance Learning.

Purcell-Gates, V., N. Duke, and J. Martineau. 2007. "Learning to Read and Write Genre-Specific Text: Roles of Authentic Experience and Explicit Teaching." *Reading Research Quarterly* 42 (1): 8–45.

Reardon, S. 2011. "The Widening Academic Achievement Gap Between the Rich and the Poor: New Evidence and Possible Explanations." In *Wither Opportunity? Rising Inequality, Schools, and Children's Life Chances*, edited by G. Duncan and R. Murname, 91–116. New York: The Russell Sage Foundation.

Renaissance Learning. 2012. *What Kids Are Reading: The Book Reading Habits of Students in American Schools*. Wisconsin Rapids, WI: Renaissance Learning.

Rich, M. 2012. "For Young Latino Readers, an Image Is Missing." *The New York Times*, December 4. Available at www.nytimes .com/2012/12/05/education/young-latino-students-dont-see-them -selves-in-books.html.

Ross, C. S., L. McKechnie, and P. Rothbauer. 2005. *Reading Matters: What the Research Reveals About Reading, Libraries, and Community.* Westport, CT: Libraries Unlimited.

Smith, C., R. Constantino, and S. Krashen. 1997. "Differences in Print Environment: Children in Beverly Hills, Compton, and Watts." *Emergency Librarian* 24: 8–9.

Vitiello, C. 2008. *Durham READS: Summer Reading Results.* Durham, NC: Metametrics.

White, T., and J. Kim. 2008. "Teacher and Parent Scaffolding of Voluntary Summer Reading." *The Reading Teacher* 62 (2): 116–25.

Williams, L. 2008. "Book Selections of Economically Disadvantaged Black Elementary Students." *Journal of Educational Research* 102 (1): 51–63.

# Don't Control Your Classroom—Manage It

*"The classroom reality is that rewards
and consequences only bring temporary
compliance at best. Human beings,
even young ones, just aren't
that easy to control."*

—Gianna Cassetta and Brook Sawyer

## No More Taking Away Recess and Other Problematic Discipline Practices

### Gianna Cassetta and Brook Sawyer

"Management and control are not the same," write teacher and school leader Gianna Cassetta and noted researcher Brook Sawyer. If trying harder to exert control is sapping your energy and burning you out, they show how to transition away from the roles of disciplinarian or goody dispenser and toward a professionally satisfying model for classroom management. Get going with:

- the rationale for abandoning reward and consequence tactics

- research on more developmentally appropriate—and efficient—management

- a plan that integrates instruction and management to decrease interruptions and increase learning

- specific strategies for addressing misbehavior on the spot and refocusing on learning goals

- ways to analyze problematic behaviors and help students get engaged and motivated.

*Grades K–5 / 978-0-325-05114-7 / 2013 / 96pp / $14.00*

 @HeinemannPub

 Visit **Heinemann.com** to order online.
To order by phone call **800.225.5800** or fax **877.231.6980**.

Prices subject to change without notice.